GARY ROBERT MUSCHLA

THE
Writing Teacher's
BOOK OF LISTS
SECOND EDITION

With Ready-to-Use Activities and Worksheets

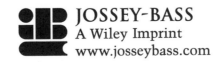

JOSSEY-BASS
A Wiley Imprint
www.josseybass.com

Published by Jossey-Bass
A Wiley Imprint
989 Market Street, San Francisco, CA 94103-1741   www.josseybass.com

The materials that appear in this book (except those for which reprint permission must be obtained from the primary sources) may be reproduced for educational/training activities. We do, however, require that the following statement appear on all reproductions:

The Writing Teacher's Book of Lists by Gary Robert Muschla.
Copyright © 2004 by Gary Robert Muschla.

This free permission is limited to the reproduction of material for educational/training events. Systematic or large-scale reproduction or distribution (more than one hundred copies per year)—or inclusion of items in publications for sale—may be done only with prior written permission. Also, reproduction on computer disk or by any other electronic means requires prior written permission. Requests for permission should be addressed to the Permissons Department, John Wiley & Sons, Inc., 111 River Street, Hoboken, NJ 07030, 201-748-6011, fax 201-748-6008, e-mail: permcoordinator@wiley.com.

Jossey-Bass books and products are available through most bookstores. To contact Jossey-Bass directly, call our Customer Care Department within the U.S. at 800-956-7739, outside the U.S. at 317-572-3986 or fax 317-572-4002.

Jossey-Bass also publishes its books in a variety of electronic formats. Some content that appears in print may not be available in electronic books.

Clip Art illustrations used by permission of Dover Publications.

ISBN 0-7879-7080-8

Printed in the United States of America

SECOND EDITION

PB Printing   10 9 8 7 6 5 4 3

CONTENTS

SECTION TWO

Lists and Activities for Nonfiction Writing

SECTION THREE

Lists and Activities for Fiction Writing

Lists and Activities for Writing Style

SECTION FIVE

Rules, Checklists, and Activities for Student Writers

SECTION SIX

Special Lists for Student Writers

SECTION SEVEN

Special Lists for Teachers

For Judy and Erin, as always

ABOUT THE AUTHOR

Gary Robert Muschla received his B.A. and M.A.T. from Trenton State College and taught at Appleby School in Spotswood, New Jersey, for more than twenty-five years. He spent many of his years in the classroom specializing in reading and language arts. In addition to his years as a classroom teacher, Mr. Muschla has been a successful writer, editor, and ghostwriter. He is a member of the Authors Guild and the National Writers Association.

Mr. Muschla has authored several other resources for teachers, including: *Writing Workshop Survival Kit* (1993), *English Teacher's Great Books Activities Kit* (1994), *Reading Workshop Survival Kit* (1997), *Ready-to-Use Reading Proficiency Lessons and Activities, 4th-Grade Level* (2002), *Ready-to-Use Reading Proficiency Lessons and Activities, 8th-Grade Level* (2002), and *Ready-to-Use Reading Proficiency Lessons and Activities, 10th-Grade Level* (2003), all published by Jossey-Bass.

With his wife, Judy, he has co-authored *The Math Teacher's Book of Lists* (1995), *Hands-on Math Projects with Real-Life Applications* (1996), *Math Starters! 5- to 10-Minute Activities to Make Kids Think, Grades 6–12* (1999), *The Geometry Teacher's Activities Kit* (2000), and *Math Smart: Ready-to-Use Activities to Motivate and Challenge Students, Grades 6–12* (2002), all published by Jossey-Bass.

Mr. Muschla currently writes and works as a consultant in education.

ACKNOWLEDGMENTS

I would like to thank my editors Steve D. Thompson, Ph.D., and Elisa Rassen for presenting me with the opportunity to update and expand the original edition of this book. Their support and guidance throughout the project is most appreciated.

Thanks also to my daughter, Erin, who, as the first reader of the manuscript, caught many of my oversights and offered several suggestions that helped me in my efforts to update the lists of this book.

Special thanks to my wife, Judy, who once again assumed the task of arranging the illustrations that liven these pages.

I appreciate the efforts of Cathy Mallon, my production editor, who managed all the steps necessary for turning this manuscript into a book.

A special thank you to Diane Turso, who proofread my work and put the final polish on it.

And finally, my thanks to my colleagues and students, who have made writing and teaching a satisfying and fulfilling experience.

ABOUT THIS BOOK

Since the publication of the first edition of this book in 1991, writing has gained full recognition as an essential skill, crucial for success in the 21st century. Fortunately, the skills necessary for competent writing can be learned and improved. While not all students may have the ability to become professional authors, almost all can acquire proficient writing skills. As a teacher of writing, it is your task to present activities and experiences that help students learn to write with clarity, confidence, and enjoyment.

The Writing Teacher's Book of Lists (second edition), therefore, has three important goals:

1. To be a resource that helps you teach writing more effectively.

2. To provide students with information and ideas that can help them improve their writing skills.

3. To provide meaningful activities that will help students develop an understanding of the writing process.

Without question, given the proper instruction and experiences, students can acquire the skills that will enable them to express themselves clearly and efficiently. I would like to extend to you my best wishes as you embark on this vital undertaking.

Gary Robert Muschla

HOW TO USE THIS BOOK

The Writing Teacher's Book of Lists (second edition) is divided into seven sections and contains a total of ninety lists. Many of the lists are accompanied by writing activities and reproducible worksheets, sublists, and background information that enhance the material of the original list. While the lists of the first edition have been updated and expanded, sixteen new lists have been added, examples of which include List 61, "Story Parts," List 66, "Common Writing Mistakes (and How to Fix Them)," and List 70, "Web Sites for Student Writers."

Following is a brief summary of each section:

Section 1, "Lists and Activities for Special Words and Word Groups," contains eleven lists that address such topics as synonyms, antonyms, hard-to-spell words, easily confused words, and words associated with time. These lists are accompanied by teaching suggestions, writing activities, and reproducible worksheets.

Section 2, "Lists and Activities for Nonfiction Writing," contains seventeen lists designed to help your students gain an understanding of the field of nonfiction. Examples of some of the topics of this section include words related to advertising, ecology, education, government and politics, newspapers and magazines, and travel. Teaching suggestions, activities, and reproducible worksheets are included with each list of this section.

Section 3, "Lists and Activities for Fiction Writing," contains eight lists designed to help your students recognize the scope of fiction. These lists focus on words related to various genres, from adventure and romance stories to westerns. Teaching suggestions, activities, and reproducible worksheets are included.

Section 4, "Lists and Activities for Writing Style," contains eight lists designed to help your students discover and polish their writing styles. Among the topics covered are alliteration, clichés, figures of speech, overblown phrases, and transitional words and phrases. Teaching suggestions, activities, and reproducible worksheets are included in this section.

Section 5, "Rules, Checklists, and Activities for Student Writers," contains fifteen lists that offer a variety of rules on capitalization, punctuation, and spelling, as well as checklists for various topics such as revision and proofreading. Teaching suggestions, activities, and reproducible worksheets accompany the lists of this section.

Section 6, "Special Lists for Student Writers," contains twenty-three lists covering an assortment of topics for students, including traits of good writers, how to find ideas for writing, common writing mistakes, guidelines for writing query letters, manuscript preparation, markets for student writers, Web sites for student writers, and ways to improve scores on writing tests.

Section 7, "Special Lists for Teachers," contains eight lists designed especially for teachers of writing. The lists address a wide range of subjects, including providing a classroom atmosphere that is conducive to writing, questions to help focus writing topics, ways to publish the writing of students, and a self-appraisal for teachers of writing.

All of the lists of the first five sections include teaching suggestions and ready-to-use writing activities. The teaching suggestions provide valuable information, methods, and techniques for teaching writing, while the activities enable your students to improve their writing skills as they apply the knowledge they gained from the lists. The lists serve to generate ideas as well as to provide vocabulary files. Because the topics of the activities focus on subjects that are familiar to students, anxiety levels are kept low, allowing students to concentrate on their writing. Reproducible worksheets provide variety and broaden the scope of the activities.

Sections 6 and 7 contain numerous reference and resource lists for students and teachers. While the lists of Section 6 are designed to support the writing efforts of your students, the lists of Section 7 are designed to support your instructional program.

Like its original edition, a major strength of this second edition of *The Writing Teacher's Book of Lists* is its flexibility and ease of implementation. The lists are designed to be used with students of various grades and abilities. Because each list stands alone, you are able to employ the materials of the book as necessary to accommodate the needs of your students. Moreover, the lists are cross-referenced so that you can refer to additional material should you wish to expand concepts or provide more information through a related topic. The book can be used either as the foundation of your writing program, or it can supplement your language arts curriculum. While working through the book in order will provide your students with a comprehensive and effective writing experience, most teachers will find that matching the lists and activities to their writing programs is the best way to use the materials of this book.

The lists, activities, and reproducible worksheets on the following pages will undoubtedly provide your students with a variety of writing experiences. This second edition of *The Writing Teacher's Book of Lists* will enhance your writing program and make your teaching of writing easier and more effective.

LISTS AND ACTIVITIES FOR

Special Words and Word Groups

Synonyms

TEACHING SUGGESTIONS

Synonyms are words that have similar meanings. An understanding of synonyms expands the vocabulary of students and can help them find precise words that clearly communicate their ideas. In discussing synonyms with your students, be sure to emphasize that dictionaries and thesauruses are good sources in which to find words that have similar meanings.

Activity 1 – Worksheet 1, "My Favorite Thing to Do"

OBJECTIVE: Students are to select one of their favorite pastimes and write a descriptive essay.

PROCEDURE: Distribute copies of List 1 and briefly review the synonyms with your students. Next, ask them to think of a favorite pastime. What do they like to do most? You might ask for volunteers to share their favorite activities and write examples on the board or an overhead projector. This will help generate ideas as well as enthusiasm.

For the assignment, hand out copies of Worksheet 1. Note that completing the worksheet will help them to organize their thoughts for writing. After they complete the worksheet, they are to write an essay describing their favorite pastime.

Activity 2 – Creating Synonym Word Finds

OBJECTIVE: Students are to create synonym word finds.

PROCEDURE: Hand out copies of List 1 and discuss synonyms with your students. For the assignment, explain that they will be making word finds that contain at least twelve words.

While students should be free to design their puzzles in any shape they wish, tell them that simple squares or rectangles are the easiest with which to work.

The words of the puzzle may run right to left, left to right, upward, downward, or diagonally. You may suggest that your students complete their word finds on computers and print their final copies, or you may pass out graph paper to facilitate the making of the puzzles.

At the bottom of the puzzle, students are to include a Word Bank. However, the words in the Word Bank will not be the words found in the puzzles. Instead, each word in the puzzle is to be a synonym of a word in the Word Bank. To find the words in the puzzle, students must first identify synonyms of the words in the Word Bank. Your students may use the synonyms of List 1, or they may use words of their own in creating their puzzles.

If you wish, you may make copies of the completed word finds and have a Synonym Word Find Event, allowing students to work out each other's puzzles. You may also decide to collect the puzzles and produce a class *Synonym Word Find Book,* and then distribute copies to students.

See List 2, "Antonyms."

Synonyms

Synonyms are words that are similar in meaning. Knowledge of synonyms enables a writer to find the words that best communicate his or her ideas. Dictionaries and thesauruses are good sources in which to find synonyms. Following are some examples.

abandon – forsake	calm – placid
about – nearly	capable – competent
act – do	capture – seize
add – attach	carry – lug
after – following	catastrophe – disaster
amazing – astounding	change – alter
ambition – aspiration	cheap – inexpensive
answer – reply	children – youngsters
approve – accept	close – shut
ask – question	clumsy – awkward
attack – assault	comfort – ease
authoritative – commanding	conscientious – responsible
automaton – robot	consent – agree
automobile – car	cramped – confined
back – rear	deal – bargain
baffle – puzzle	distrustful – suspicious
barren – infertile	dull – dim
barrier – obstacle	dumb – stupid
before – prior to	eat – consume
betray – reveal	elaborate – complex
bewilder – confuse	elastic – flexible
bitter – stinging	end – finish
bored – indifferent	enormous – gigantic
boss – supervisor	enough – sufficient
brave – valiant	every – all
bright – brilliant	fight – battle
brook – creek	flaw – defect
buddy – friend	food – nourishment
build – construct	forgive – pardon
call – summon	form – shape

Synonyms *(continued)*

fundamental – basic

funny – comical

fury – rage

gift – present

give – grant

goal – objective

good – suitable

great – grand

grow – mature

hard – rigid

have – possess

help – assist

high – lofty

idea – concept

impolite – rude

incident – occurrence

incline – slant

incredible – unbelievable

join – unite

just – fair

kind – gentle

large – big

learn – understand

like – enjoy

little – small

long – lengthy

lovely – beautiful

man – male

mild – gentle

mistake – error

nation – country

naughty – bad

nautical – marine

near – close

neat – orderly

new – recent

nimble – agile

now – immediately

ocean – sea

often – frequently

old – ancient

ominous – threatening

one – single

pain – ache

part – portion

pensive – thoughtful

picture – image

place – spot

plain – simple

play – frolic

power – strength

precious – valuable

primary – main

push – shove

put – set

quake – tremble

quick – rapid

reason – infer

refuse – reject

relate – tell

restriction – limitation

right – correct

roar – bellow

say – state

seem – appear

shortened – abbreviated

show – display

start – begin

stop – cease

strong – sturdy

study – examine

suggest – advise

summit – peak

supply – provide

sure – certain

surprise – astound

tasty – delicious

teach – instruct

thin – slender

think – consider

time – period

tired – weary

tough – hardy

tricky – clever

uncommon – unusual

under – below

universe – cosmos

unlike – different

unwise – foolish

use – utilize

usual – ordinary

vacant – empty

vague – unclear

vain – conceited

valley – glen

vast – huge

verge – edge

vital – essential

vow – swear

want – desire

while – during

word – term

work – labor

world – globe

worry – anxiety

wrestle – grapple

write – record

yank – pull

zenith – summit

zero – nothing

My Favorite Thing to Do

DIRECTIONS: Think of a favorite pastime, something you really enjoy doing. Answer the questions that follow, then write a descriptive essay of your favorite pastime.

1. What is your favorite pastime? _____

   _____

   _____

   _____

   _____

2. Write five words that describe your pastime, then write two synonyms for each. _____

   _____

   _____

   _____

   _____

   _____

   _____

3. How did you learn about this pastime? _____

   _____

   _____

   _____

   _____

4. Why do you enjoy this pastime? _____

   _____

   _____

   _____

   _____

   _____

2

Antonyms

TEACHING SUGGESTIONS

Antonyms are words that are opposite in meaning. A basic understanding of antonyms not only broadens vocabulary, but is also helpful in descriptions and making comparisons between different things. Sometimes a student can find the exact word he or she needs to describe an idea by thinking of its opposite first.

In teaching antonyms, point out to your students that dictionaries and thesauruses are sources they can consult when they need information about antonyms.

Activity 1 – Worksheet 2, "A Matter of Character"

OBJECTIVE: Students are to select a hero or villain and write a description of this person's opposite.

PROCEDURE: Distribute List 2 and discuss antonyms with your students. Explain that writers rely heavily on opposites. Almost every story, for example, is built around the conflict between opposites—the hero and the villain.

Next, ask your students to name some heroes and villains. They may name real people, historical figures, or characters from fiction. Discuss some of the traits of heroes and villains, which you might list on the board or an overhead projector. Note how the traits of heroes and villains differ, and explain that writers use such distinctive traits to create their characters.

Hand out copies of Worksheet 2. Instruct your students to select a hero or villain and answer the questions on the worksheet. Note that through the use of antonyms they will be changing heroes to villains and villains to heroes. They are to write a description of this new character.

EXTENSION: After students have written their descriptions, they may write a story about the new character they have created.

Activity 2 – Creating Antonym Crossword Puzzles

OBJECTIVE: Students are to create antonym crossword puzzles.

PROCEDURE: Hand out copies of List 2 and discuss antonyms with your students. Explain that they will be creating antonym crossword puzzles.

The puzzles are to contain at least twelve words. You may hand out graph paper to facilitate the making of the puzzles, or, if students have access to puzzle-making software, they may create their puzzles on computers and then print their final puzzles. (Not only do a variety of vendors offer puzzle-making software, but a search on the Internet with the key words "puzzle makers" will yield numerous web sites, many of which have free puzzle-making capabilities.)

In the puzzles required for this assignment, each clue is to be an antonym of a word in the puzzle. Thus, to find the words in the puzzle, your students must first identify antonyms. While you may permit students to use the antonyms from List 2, choosing other words, especially words that have multiple antonyms, will make the puzzles more challenging.

You may wish to make copies of the puzzles and allow students to complete them, or you may compile the puzzles in a class *Antonym Crossword Puzzle Book.*

See List 1, "Synonyms."

Antonyms

Antonyms are words that have opposite or nearly opposite meanings. Sometimes authors can find the precise word they need by thinking of its opposite first. Following are common antonyms. You can find many more by consulting your dictionary or thesaurus.

above – below	curiosity – indifference
add – subtract	curtail – increase
after – before	day – night
alive – dead	defeat – victory
all – none	deny – affirm
allow – prohibit	downcast – happy
answer – question	dull – bright
apart – together	even – odd
arrive – leave	fast – slow
ask – tell	father – mother
away – toward	find – lose
back – front	first – last
ban – approve	forbid – permit
barbaric – civilized	friend – enemy
bashful – bold	general – specific
beautiful – ugly	gentle – brutal
begin – end	gloomy – cheerful
bored – enthusiastic	good – bad
breezy – calm	great – unimportant
careless – cautious	group – individual
child – adult	hard – soft
closed – open	help – hurt
cold – hot	hero – villain
common – exceptional	hide – reveal
costly – cheap	high – low
courageous – cowardly	inferior – superior
create – destroy	innocent – guilty
critic – supporter	kind – cruel
crooked – straight	knowledge – ignorance
crowded – empty	left – right

Antonyms *(continued)*

life – death

light – dark

little – big

long – short

loose – tight

many – few

mean – kind

moist – dry

more – less

move – stay

much – little

nasty – nice

near – far

neat – messy

neglect – cherish

nervous – calm

never – always

nothing – everything

now – then

obscure – clear

often – seldom

other – same

outside – inside

part – whole

pause – continue

polite – rude

positive – negative

problem – solution

profit – loss

proud – humble

refuse – permit

remember – forget

right – wrong

safe – dangerous

same – different

send – receive

shallow – deep

sharp – blunt

simple – complex

small – large

smooth – rough

start – stop

stingy – generous

strong – weak

take – give

tall – short

that – this

there – here

to – from

under – over

up – down

wealthy – poor

young – old

A Matter of Character

DIRECTIONS: Consider some of your favorite heroes or villains in stories you have read or seen on TV or in the movies. Choose a hero or villain, answer the questions below, and write a character sketch of his or her opposite.

1. Who is the hero or villain you have selected? _____

   _____

   _____

2. In what story did this character appear? _____

   _____

   _____

3. Describe your hero or villain. _____

   _____

   _____

   _____

   _____

4. What is this character's most dominant trait? _____

   _____

   _____

   _____

   _____

5. List the traits this character's opposite would possess. _____

   _____

   _____

   _____

   _____

   _____

Homographs

TEACHING SUGGESTIONS

Homographs are words that have the same spelling but different meanings and origins. Sometimes their pronunciations vary as well. While this may not present a major problem in writing (*līv* and *liv* are both spelled *l-i-v-e*), emphasize that homographs can cause slip-ups when students give a speech or presentation.

Use the word *invalid* (*in-val'-id*) as an example. If a student is giving a talk on acid rain, he or she might conclude that some of the early theories of how acid rain forms are *in-val'-id* in the light of current evidence. However, if the student says they are *in'-val-id,* he or she is likely to draw chuckles instead of serious consideration.

Activity 1 – Worksheet 3, "The Concert"

OBJECTIVE: Students are to identify the correct homographs in a story.

PROCEDURE: Hand out List 3 and discuss homographs. Next, distribute Worksheet 3 and instruct your students to read the story. They are to choose the correct homograph, based on pronunciation, from each pair of words. When your students have completed the worksheet, you may wish to go over it orally with them.

ANSWER KEY: līv, prez'-ent, min'-it, lēd, clōs, wīnd, kon-tent', bās

Activity 2 – The Event

OBJECTIVE: Students are to write an account of a special event they attended.

PROCEDURE: Ask your students to think of a time they attended a concert; a baseball, football, or soccer game; or another major event. Instruct them to write about this experience. Encourage them to answer the questions *who, what, when, where, why,* and *how* in their writing. Also encourage them to note any homographs they used.
    See List 4, "Homophones," and List 7, "Easily Confused Words."

Homographs

Homographs are words that are spelled the same but have different meanings and origins. In many cases, homographs have the same pronunciation. *Hide* (*hīd*), meaning "to keep out of sight," is pronounced the same as *hide,* which means "the skin of an animal." Some homographs, however, are pronounced differently. *Invalid* (*in'-val-id*), meaning "a bedridden person," is spoken with the accent on the first syllable, while *invalid* (*in-val'-id*), meaning "not valid or unacceptable," has the accent on the second syllable. The following list offers a varied assortment of some of the more common homographs of the English language, including pronunciations for those that are spoken differently.

angle – a figure formed when two lines meet at a point

angle – to fish with rod, line, and hook

arms – limbs extending from shoulders to hand

arms – weapons

august (aw gust') – inspiring admiration

August (aw'-gust) – the eighth month of the year

ball – a formal dance

ball – a round object

bank – a long mound or heap (snow, ground, and so forth)

bank – a place where financial transactions are conducted

bank – the edge of a stream or lake

bear – a large animal

bear – to support or carry

boil – a local inflammation of the skin

boil – to bring to a seething bubbling state by heating

buck – a dollar (slang)

buck – a male deer

can – a metal container

can – to be able to

chop – the jaw of an animal

chop – to cut

close (klōs) – nearby

close (klōz) – to shut

content (kon'-tent) – a thing that is contained

content (kon-tent') – pleased, satisfied

count – a title of nobility

count – to number

cue – a long, tapering stick used in a game of pool

cue – a signal

date – a sweet fruit of the Eastern date palm

date – the time of an event

duck – a broad-beaked, web-footed water bird

duck – a coarse cloth used for small sails and clothing

duck – to dip suddenly

fan – a devoted admirer

fan – a machine used to produce currents of air

flat – a small apartment

flat – level

Homographs *(continued)*

fleet – a group of ships

fleet – fast, rapid

fresh – disrespectful

fresh – new

grave – a burial site

grave – of great importance

hamper – a large covered basket or container

hamper – to hinder the movement of

haze – a light suspension of particles in the air

haze – to subject to pranks

hide – the skin of an animal

hide – to keep out of sight

invalid (in'-val-id) – a bedridden person

invalid (in-val'-id) – not valid, unacceptable

jar – a container of glass or earthenware

jar – to cause to vibrate by sudden impact

kind – a class or grouping

kind – friendly, sympathetic

lark – a small bird

lark – to play or frolic

like – similar

like – to be pleased with

minute (mī-nüt') – very small

minute (min'-it) – sixty seconds

miss – an unmarried woman or girl

miss – fail to hit

moor – a marshy wasteland

moor – to secure a ship by anchors or cables

nag – an old horse

nag – to scold

pitcher – a baseball player

pitcher – a container for pouring liquids

poker – a card game

poker – a metal rod for stirring a fire

pupil – a student

pupil – part of the eye

quack – one who pretends to have skill in medicine

quack – the sound of a duck

rare – meat cooked in a short time

rare – uncommon

rash – an eruption on the skin

rash – hasty

ray – a flat fish

ray – a narrow beam of light

saw – a hand tool for cutting

saw – past tense of *see*

school – a group of fish

school – an institution for learning

scrap – a fight

scrap – a small piece of something

sock – a short stocking

sock – to hit hard

soil – ground or dirt

soil – to make dirty

spell – a period of time

spell – an enchantment

spell – to say or write the letters of a word

Homographs *(continued)*

tear (târ) – to rip apart

tear (tir) – a drop of fluid from the eye

tire – a hoop of rubber placed around a wheel

tire – to become weary

wake – to rouse from sleep

wake – waves following a ship

wind (wind) – moving air

wind (wīnd) – to turn or twist around

yard – a measure of length equal to three feet

yard – an area surrounding a building

The Concert

DIRECTIONS: Read the following story and circle the correct homographs from the pairs of words.

Last night, my three best friends and I went to a concert. We saw my favorite group (liv, līv). I have every CD and song they ever recorded. It was the biggest surprise of my life when my parents gave me the tickets for my birthday (prez'-ent, pri-zent').

As the day of the concert approached, it seemed that I counted every (mī-nüt', min'-it). When the day finally arrived, we left home early because there were no reserved seats.

As soon as we got to the concert, which was held in a park, I took the (led, lēd) and went directly to the main gate. I wanted to get as (clōs, clōz) to the front as possible. I tried to (wind, wīnd) my way to the stage, but it was too crowded. We had to settle toward the back, but I was (kon-tent', kon'-tent) to simply listen to the music. Although each member of the group is an accomplished singer, I feel that John, who sings (bās, bas), is the best.

4

Homophones

TEACHING SUGGESTIONS

Homophones are words that have the same sound but different spellings, meanings, and origins. They are easy to misuse, and they creep into all forms of writing. Becoming familiar with common homophones is the best way to avoid making mistakes with them.

Activity 1 – Worksheet 4, "Jennifer's Party"

OBJECTIVE: Students are to identify the correct homophones in a story.

PROCEDURE: Distribute copies of List 4 and discuss homophones. Next, hand out copies of Worksheet 4. Instruct your students to read the story and circle the correct homophones from the pairs of words. When your students have completed the worksheet, you may wish to go over it orally.

ANSWER KEY: allowed, wait, great, knew, pray, sun, one, hair, eight, here, patience, clothes, weather, break

Activity 2 – Weathered Event

OBJECTIVE: Students are to write about an event that was negatively affected by the weather.

PROCEDURE: After your students have finished Worksheet 4, ask them if, like Jennifer, they had ever planned a special event and the weather spoiled the occasion. Instruct them to write an account of this time. (For students who have never had an event ruined by bad weather, suggest that they write an ending to "Jennifer's Party" instead.) Remind your students to pay close attention to their use of homophones.

See List 3, "Homographs," and List 7, "Easily Confused Words."

Homophones

Homophones are words that sound the same but have different spellings, meanings, and origins. They are easy to misuse. The following list contains common homophones.

air – the atmosphere
heir – a successor to property or rank

allowed – permitted
aloud – with a loud voice

altar – a raised structure used for worship
alter – to change

ate – past tense of *eat*
eight – a number

ball – a round object
bawl – to cry or shout

band – a musical group
banned – prohibited

base – the bottom part
bass – the lowest pitched male singing voice

be – to exist
bee – a flying insect

beach – shore
beech – a type of tree

blew – past tense of *blow*
blue – the color of the clear, daytime sky

bough – a tree limb
bow – the forward part of a ship

brake – a device for slowing or stopping a vehicle
break – to crack or split

buy – to purchase
by – close or near
bye – short for *goodbye*

canvas – a type of cloth
canvass – to survey

capital – money available for investment
capitol – the building in which a state government meets

cell – a basic unit of life
sell – to trade for money

cent – a hundredth part of a dollar
scent – a smell
sent – past tense of *send*

cereal – food made from grains
serial – a story presented in installments

chews – to bite and crush with teeth
choose – to select

chord – a combination of tones sounded together
cord – a thick string or thin rope

cite – to bring forth as proof
sight – the ability to perceive with the eyes
site – a place

coarse – rough
course – the way covered

council – an assembly
counsel – to give advice

dear – highly valued

deer – an animal

die – to cease living

dye – substance used to color materials

dual – two

duel – combat between two individuals

earn – to gain something through work

urn – a container

fir – a type of evergreen tree

fur – the hair covering the body of some
　　animals

flea – a tiny insect

flee – to run away

flew – past tense of *fly*

flu – the short form of *influenza,* a viral
　　infection

flue – a duct in a chimney

forth – forward in place or time

fourth – next after third

foul – filthy

fowl – a domesticated bird such as a chicken

grate – to rub and produce a harsh sound

great – enormous, wonderful, or magnificent

hair – a filament growing from the skin of
　　an animal

hare – a rabbit

hangar – a building for storing airplanes

hanger – a device from which to hang
　　something

heal – to restore to health

heel – the back part of the bottom of the foot

he'll – contraction for *he will*

hear – to perceive with the ear

here – in this spot

heard – past tense of *hear*

herd – a group of animals

hi – a greeting

hie – to hurry

high – far up, tall

hoarse – harsh or husky sounding

horse – a large animal

hole – an opening

whole – entire, complete

hour – sixty minutes

our – belonging to us

knew – past tense of *know*

new – not existing before the present time

knight – a soldier of feudal times

night – the time of darkness between day-
　　light and sunset

knot – an intertwining of rope or string

not – in no way

know – to be aware of

no – a negative reply

lead – a heavy metal

led – past tense of *lead,* meaning *to guide*

lessen – to decrease

lesson – something to be learned

loan – to lend, or something that is lent

lone – single, solitary

made – past tense of *make*

maid – a female domestic servant

Homophones *(continued)*

main – of great importance

Maine – a Northeastern state

mane – the long hair on the neck of an animal

might – power, strength

mite – a small insect

none – not any

nun – a woman in a religious order

oar – a type of paddle used to propel a boat

or – a conjunction that introduces an alternative

ore – a mineral deposit

one – the lowest cardinal number

won – past tense of *win*

pail – a bucket

pale – faint in color

pain – distress or suffering

pane – glass in a window

patience – the ability to endure things calmly

patients – people being treated for health problems

peace – calmness

piece – a part of something

peal – to ring

peel – to remove a covering

peer – an equal

pier – a dock

pray – to worship

prey – an animal hunted and killed for food

principal – most important in rank

principle – a fundamental law or truth

rain – condensed moisture falling from clouds

reign – the period during which a ruler maintains authority

rein – a leather strap used to control a horse

read – past tense of *read*

red – the color of blood

real – genuine

reel – a spool

right – proper

rite – a religious practice

write – to set down in letters or words on paper

root – part of a plant that grows underground

route – a course or way

rose – a flowering bush

rows – lines

sail – a sheet of canvas used to catch the wind to move a boat

sale – an exchange of goods or services for money

sane – having a sound mind

seine – an open net used for fishing

sea – an ocean (or a part of an ocean)

see – to perceive with the eyes

sew – to mend

so – in such manner

sow – to plant

slay – to kill

sleigh – a large sled, typically drawn by horses

soar – to fly high

sore – painful

sole – the flat bottom part of the foot

soul – the spiritual part of a human being

some – a part of

sum – a total

son – a male child

sun – the star around which the Earth revolves

stake – a sharpened stick or post

steak – a slice of beef

stationary – not moving

stationery – writing paper

steal – to rob

steel – a strong metal made by mixing carbon and iron

straight – passing from one point directly to another

strait – a narrow channel of water joining two bodies of water

suite – a series of connected rooms

sweet – sugary

tail – a flexible extension of an animal's spine

tale – a story

team – a group of people working together for a common goal

teem – to be stocked to overflowing

tear – a drop of fluid from the eye

tier – a series of level rows arranged above each other

their – possessive pronoun meaning *of them*

there – in that place

they're – contraction for *they are*

to – in a direction toward

too – also

two – the sum of one and one

vain – conceited

vane – a device that shows the direction of the wind

vein – a blood vessel

vial – a small bottle

vile – disgusting, revolting

waist – the part of the body below the ribs and above the hips

waste – to use foolishly

wait – to stay

weight – the amount of heaviness

ware – an article of merchandise

wear – to carry clothes on one's body

where – at what place

weak – feeble

week – seven successive days

weather – the state of the atmosphere

whether – if

which – who or what one

witch – a sorceress

who's – contraction for *who is*

whose – possessive pronoun meaning *of whom*

your – pronoun meaning *of you*

you're – contraction for *you are*

Jennifer's Party

DIRECTIONS: Read the following story and circle the correct homophones from the pairs of words.

Jennifer's mother (allowed, aloud) Jennifer to have a party for her birthday. Jennifer could hardly (wait, weight).

"Oh, Mom," she said, "it's going to be (grate, great). I just hope it doesn't snow. You know how bad February can be."

"That's true," said her mother, "but it can just as easily be a nice day."

Unfortunately for Jennifer, when the day of her party came, the sky was cloudy and the forecast called for snow. Looking out the window at the dark clouds, Jennifer (new, knew) her party would be ruined. She started to (prey, pray) for the (son, sun) to shine.

"Mom, what will we do if it snows and no (one, won) comes?" she said as she combed her (hare, hair).

"Your friends will come," her mother said.

"Well, I just wish it was (eight, ate) o'clock already and everybody was (hear, here)," Jennifer said.

"You must have (patients, patience)," her mother said, smiling.

As Jennifer put on her party (clothes, close), the snow began. The (weather, whether) report said that it was likely to snow all night.

"Oh, no," Jennifer said, ready to (brake, break) into tears.

5

Hard-to-Spell Words
(Intermediate)

TEACHING SUGGESTIONS

Spelling in the English language is best described as inconsistent. Whereas some words are spelled the way they sound, many are not. Even when you follow spelling rules, you are confronted by exceptions. Nevertheless, spelling is an important subject. Correct spelling is essential to written communication, and spelling assessments are common in both standardized and classroom tests.

Since many of the words of List 5 appear on standardized tests, you might use them to augment your regular spelling assignments in preparation for testing. You can take groups of ten, fifteen, or twenty words each week and have your students learn their spellings and meanings. You can then test the students yourself or have them test each other.

To help your students remember the spellings of new words, encourage them to pay close attention to spelling and incorporate new words in their writing and speaking. (This will also foster the development of their vocabularies.) Suggest that they maintain lists of words that they find hard to spell (see Activity 2), consult dictionaries whenever they are unsure of the correct spelling of a word, and use the spelling checker whenever they are writing with computers.

Activity 1 – Worksheet 5, "A Time of Great Emotion"

OBJECTIVE: Students are to write an account of an emotional event; they are to use at least twenty of the words of List 5.

PROCEDURE: Hand out copies of List 5 and briefly review the list with your students. Next, distribute copies of Worksheet 5 and ask your students to think of a specific time their emotions were great, or even out of control. This may have been a frightening, frustrating, or exciting event. Instruct your students to answer the questions on the worksheet in preparation of writing and then write an account of this event. In their accounts they are to use at least twenty words of List 5.

Activity 2 – Maintaining Personal Spelling Lists

OBJECTIVE: Students are to develop and maintain personal spelling lists of hard-to-spell words.

PROCEDURE: After distributing and briefly reviewing List 5, explain that many people have trouble with spelling. Since many of us regularly misspell the same words, maintaining personal lists of words we find particularly hard to spell can be helpful.

Instruct your students to set aside a section of a spiral notebook and write down any words that they find hard to spell. Emphasize that they should write the words in rough alphabetical order, leaving plenty of space between them so that more words can be included later.

Explain that when they are writing, they should keep a copy of their personal spelling lists handy and refer to the list as necessary.

See List 6, "Hard-to-Spell Words (Advanced)," List 9, "Compound Words," and List 49, "Spelling Rules."

Hard-to-Spell Words (Intermediate)

All of us have trouble spelling some words, and many of us tend to misspell the same words over and over again. Keeping a list of hard-to-spell words like these handy can help you avoid spelling mistakes in your writing.

a lot	been	courage	eraser
ability	believe	cousin	erosion
aboard	beware	critical	estimate
absence	bicycle	cruel	excellent
achieve	billion	culture	exhale
address	blizzard	cyclone	exist
adventure	bought	decorate	exit
advice	break	describe	expensive
again	brought	desperate	experience
against	budget	didn't	explain
all right	built	different	extinct
along	bureau	disagree	factor
already	business	discuss	famine
although	chemical	distance	feather
ancestor	children	distribute	February
argue	chocolate	doctor	fertile
arithmetic	choose	dolphin	fiction
article	climate	doubt	fierce
assembly	close	doughnut	figure
autumn	closet	early	first
aware	collect	echo	Friday
awhile	comfortable	educate	friend
bacon	compare	eighth	fuel
badge	conserve	either	galaxy
bakery	continent	elevator	garage
balloon	cough	emergency	government
bargain	could	employ	guard
beagle	couldn't	enough	guess
beautiful	country	entrance	habit
because	county	envelope	Halloween

Hard-to-Spell Words (Intermediate) *(continued)*

hamburger	language	piece	several
handkerchief	latter	please	shoes
handle	laughter	plumber	shudder
harmony	lawyer	poem	silent
haven't	league	poison	since
hazard	little	popular	sincerely
headquarters	loose	practice	singular
heard	loving	pretty	skiing
hearth	machine	principal	skis
height	magic	principle	soldier
hello	maybe	profession	something
history	memory	property	sometimes
hoarse	minute	quarter	soon
hockey	Monday	quiet	special
honor	morning	quit	sprinkle
hospital	motor	quite	stairway
hour	mysterious	raise	steak
house	negative	read	stomach
human	neither	receive	straight
illustrate	nonsense	recreation	strength
imagine	o'clock	remember	studying
immediately	often	repair	substitute
increase	once	respect	sugar
independent	operation	rhyme	summer
instance	opinion	right	Sunday
instead	opposite	rough	suppose
interest	organize	route	supreme
interview	outside	sandwich	surely
it's	package	Saturday	surface
its	party	scene	surprise
janitor	patience	schedule	surround
junior	patient	school	swimming
knew	peace	separate	system
know	people	sergeant	teacher
laid	photograph	serious	telescope

Hard-to-Spell Words (Intermediate) *(continued)*

terrible	together	understand	weigh
Thanksgiving	tomorrow	universe	were
their	tonight	until	where
themselves	too	vacant	which
there	tornado	vacation	whole
they'll	tragic	vegetable	write
they're	traveling	victim	wrote
though	trouble	wear	yield
thought	truly	we're	you're
through	Tuesday	weather	your
Thursday	twelfth	Wednesday	zero

A Time of Great Emotion

DIRECTIONS: Think of a time you were frightened, frustrated, or excited. Answer the questions below, then write an account of this event. Use at least 20 words from List 5 in your writing.

1. What was this event? _____

_____

_____

_____

2. When and where did this event take place? _____

_____

_____

_____

3. Who else, besides you, was involved in this event? _____

_____

_____

_____

4. Describe the event. _____

_____

_____

_____

5. Why were your emotions so great at this time? _____

_____

_____

_____

6. How did the event end? _____

_____

_____

_____

6

Hard-to-Spell Words
(Advanced)

TEACHING SUGGESTIONS

As the words of the English language become longer, they generally become harder to spell. Students (and adults) are regularly confused by silent vowels, dropped letters, consonant blends that defy the logic of pronunciation (*gh* in *laugh* and *ph* in *phone,* for instance), and some words that are not spoken at all as they should be, such as *colonel.* Along with the words of List 6, it is not unusual for advanced students to have trouble with some of the words of the intermediate list, and you should use both lists according to the needs of your classes.

While teaching spelling to students, keep in mind that some students are and always will be weak spellers. Avoid linking poor spelling with general intelligence or the ability to write well; Ernest Hemingway was a notoriously bad speller. Your purpose should be to help your students realize that, if they have a spelling weakness, they can take steps to compensate for it.

One step, obviously, is to use the dictionary, not just for class but whenever they are unsure of the correct spelling of a word. Another step is to make a list of words that they find particularly vexing. Third, through careful editing, there need be few, if any, spelling mistakes on any written work. Finally, when your students are writing with computers, they should always use the spelling checker.

Activity 1 – Worksheet 6, "The Day I Met . . ."

OBJECTIVES: Students are to write an imaginary story about a meeting with a celebrity of their choice. They are then to act as editors and proofread a partner's story for spelling errors.

PROCEDURE: Hand out copies of List 6 and review the words with your students. Next, hand out copies of Worksheet 6 and ask your students to imagine this situation: They are able to meet with a celebrity or other well-known individual of their choice.

This individual might be a movie or TV star, a professional athlete, politician, business tycoon, or religious leader. Instruct your students to complete the worksheet and write about this imaginary meeting.

After your students have completed their drafts, instruct them to exchange their work with a partner. Partners then act as editors and proofread each other's writing, circling any spelling errors. Suggest that students refer to List 6 as well as dictionaries for help with proofreading. (Depending on your class, you may find it beneficial to also hand out copies of List 5.)

Upon completion of editing, the writers should go on to finish the final copy of their papers.

EXTENSION: You can extend this activity by using it as a springboard for students to develop personal spelling lists. Students should write in their notebooks, in rough alphabetical order, words that they found difficult to spell, leaving space between each entry so that they can add new words as necessary. These personal spelling lists should be kept handy for reference during every writing assignment.

Activity 2 – Spelling Bee with a Twist

OBJECTIVE: Students are to participate in a spelling bee.

PROCEDURE: Divide your class into teams of two or three. Older students may at first be amused by the idea of a spelling bee, but as you explain the rules, their interest and sense of competition will likely be stimulated.

Compile enough words so that each team has five opportunities to spell words. Thus, if you have ten teams, you will need at least fifty different words. You may use the words from Lists 5 or 6 as well as words from your class's reading or spelling vocabulary. The words should be new to the students, however, and should be at the upper levels of their vocabularies. This is the reason for the teams. Because the words are new, students will have the chance to confer to decide on the correct spelling.

Be sure that the words are randomly mixed, then start by saying the first word twice to the first team. You may repeat it once if necessary. The members of the team then have time to decide on the correct spelling. You should limit this time to no more than 30 seconds. Teams have one chance to spell the word before you move on to the next word and the next team. Even if the first team spells the word incorrectly, the next team receives a new word. This prevents the following team from having additional time to decide on the correct spelling. *Note:* Even though a team may spell a word incorrectly, they remain in the game. The game continues until all the words have been used.

Points are scored by spelling a word correctly, one point for each word. At the end of the round (each team having had a chance to spell five words), you can take the top two or three teams and have a playoff. You should have a fresh list of words for this. You might need five or six words for each team before a winner is declared.

If your school has a school newspaper or a PTA newsletter, be sure that the names of the winners are included in the next issue. You might also put the names of the winners on a bulletin board in a Winner's Circle Display.

This activity can generate much enthusiasm. It offers students the opportunity to have fun with spelling, while underscoring the importance of spelling words correctly.

See List 5, "Hard-to-Spell Words (Intermediate)," List 9, "Compound Words," and List 49, "Spelling Rules."

Hard-to-Spell Words (Advanced)

The words in the following list are often misspelled by students and adults. Unfortunately, many of these words appear regularly in routine written communication, as well as on many standardized tests.

abrupt	architect	caution	definitely
absurd	arctic	celebrity	delectable
acceptable	argument	cemetery	deliberate
accommodate	arrange	changeable	dependent
accumulate	athlete	chronicle	descendant
accustom	atrocious	collapse	descent
ache	attentive	colonel	description
acknowledge	audible	colossal	desert
acquaintance	augment	commemorate	despondent
acquire	authority	committee	dessert
acquittal	autonomy	comparative	devastating
adequate	awkward	concede	dignity
adolescent	bargain	conceive	dilemma
advantageous	beautician	condemn	diligence
advice	believable	condense	disagree
aisle	bellow	conscience	disastrous
allegiance	beneficial	conscientious	discipline
amateur	bilingual	conscious	disclose
ambiguous	boredom	consequence	disease
analyze	boundary	conspicuous	distinction
anonymous	breathe	contemplate	distress
anticipate	brevity	continuous	disturbance
antidote	brilliant	controversy	dominant
anxiety	briny	council	dubious
apparent	bulletin	counsel	dynamic
appearance	calendar	counterfeit	eccentric
appetizer	captivating	courtesy	edible
appreciate	career	crescent	effective
apprehension	catastrophe	criticize	efficient
approximate	category	curiosity	embarrass

embellish	humorous	justification	obedience
emigrate	hysterical	knowledge	obligation
endeavor	illiterate	laudable	obstacle
enigmatic	immune	legislate	occasion
environment	impartial	leisure	occurrence
erroneous	impeccable	liable	opportunity
especially	implication	license	optimism
esteem	important	lieutenant	opulence
estuary	impossible	literal	original
exaggerate	impressive	loathe	outrageous
except	improbable	logical	parallel
excessive	impulsive	magnificent	paralyze
exercise	inconspicuous	majestic	particular
exorbitant	incorruptible	maneuver	perceptible
extensive	incredible	marriage	perseverance
extraordinary	indecision	mathematics	personnel
faculty	independence	meager	perspiration
fallacy	informative	medicine	pessimism
familiar	inquisitive	mediocre	politics
fascinate	insufficient	melancholy	possession
feasible	intelligent	menace	preference
fiery	interesting	merit	prejudice
foreign	interfere	meticulous	prescription
foreseeable	interpret	miniature	prestige
furious	interrupt	minimum	prevalent
gaiety	invigorate	miraculous	privilege
gauge	involve	miscellaneous	probably
generous	irrelevant	mischief	procedure
grammar	isolation	nausea	professor
guarantee	itinerant	necessary	prominent
guidance	jealousy	negligence	propaganda
harassment	jewelry	negotiate	propensity
hesitate	journalist	niece	proprietor
humanity	jubilant	noticeable	pummel
humidity	judicial	nuisance	quadrant

Hard-to-Spell Words (Advanced) *(continued)*

quantity	significant	tangible	vacuum
questionnaire	similar	technique	validation
receipt	society	temperament	variegate
recommend	sophomore	tenacious	vengeance
repetition	spacious	territory	verdict
restaurant	strenuous	thorough	vigor
reverberate	subtle	translucent	villain
rhythm	sultry	transparent	visible
saucer	supercede	unanimous	wreckage
seize	susceptible	unilateral	wrench
sensible	suspicious	unnecessary	yacht

The Day I Met . . .

DIRECTIONS: Imagine that you can meet a famous person of your choice. This might be a movie or TV star, a professional athlete, a politician, a business tycoon, or a religious leader. Answer the questions below and write an account of this imaginary meeting.

1. Who would you meet? _____

   _____

2. Why did you choose this person? _____

   _____

   _____

   _____

   _____

3. When would you meet? _____

   _____

   _____

4. Where would you meet? _____

   _____

   _____

5. What would you do? _____

   _____

   _____

   _____

6. What would you talk about? _____

   _____

   _____

   _____

   _____

7

Easily Confused Words

TEACHING SUGGESTIONS

Many words in the English language sound so much alike that they are easily confused. How many times have you seen *affect* and *effect* interchanged? What about *later* and *latter*? *Passed* and *past*? If you are like most teachers, you have probably circled mistakes like these far more than you care to remember.

Since there is no set of rules you can give your students to ensure that they use the words on List 7 correctly, your teaching strategy should focus on making students aware of these words and encouraging them to consult dictionaries whenever they are doubtful of a specific usage.

The following activity will help your students become familiar with common, easily confused words.

Activity 1 – Worksheet 7, "Spaceman in the Backyard"

OBJECTIVE: Given a story containing pairs of easily confused words, students are to choose the correct word from each pair.

PROCEDURE: Distribute copies of List 7 and review the pairs of easily confused words with your students. Emphasize that such words are often interchanged, even though their meanings are quite different.

Next, hand out copies of Worksheet 7. Instruct your students to read the story and circle the correct word from each pair of easily confused words. You may permit students to use List 7 or a dictionary as they complete the worksheet.

After your students have finished the worksheet, you may wish to go over it orally and answer any questions they may have.

ANSWER KEY: bizarre, illusion, beside, close, respectfully, assistance, lightning, quite, Then, device, confident, through

Activity 2 – The Day I Met an Alien

OBJECTIVE: Students are to write a fantasy about a time they met a visitor from another planet.

PROCEDURE: Hand out copies of List 7 and review the words with your students. Ask them to imagine that they have met an alien. Where did they meet him/her/it? How did the alien arrive on Earth? How did they communicate? What did they say? What happened? How did the alien return to his/her/its home planet? Or did he/she/it remain here?

Instruct your students to write an imaginary story about their meeting with this alien. Remind them to pay close attention to any easily confused words they may use in their stories.

See List 3, "Homographs," and List 4, "Homophones."

Easily Confused Words

Because it has borrowed words from so many other languages, English is one of the richest languages in the world. We have words for just about everything. We have homographs, words that are spelled alike but have different meanings. We have homophones, words that sound alike but have different meanings. And we have words that simply sound similar. All of this, of course, makes a maddening assortment of easily confused words, some of the most common of which follow.

accede – to agree
exceed – to go beyond the limit

accept – to receive
except – to leave out

access – a way of approach
excess – that which surpasses a limit

ad – an advertisement
add – to find the sum of

adapt – to adjust
adept – proficient
adopt – to take, or accept, by choice

advice – an offered opinion or suggestion
advise – to give advice to

affect – to act upon
effect – a result

all ready – prepared; set
already – before this time

all together – everything (or everyone) in one place
altogether – entirely

alley – a passageway between buildings
alloy – a mixture of two or more metals
ally – to form an alliance

allot – to divide according to parts or shares
a lot – many

allusion – an indirect hint
illusion – an unreal image

among – mixed with
between – in the middle of two

angel – a heavenly spirit
angle – figure formed by two straight lines diverging from a point

annual – yearly
annul – to void

appraise – to place a value on
apprise – to inform

ascent – the act of rising
assent – to agree

assistance – help
assistants – helpers

attendance – the act of being present at a specific place

attendants – people who are present, usually to serve

bazaar – a fair

bizarre – odd or strange

beside – at the side of

besides – in addition

biannual – happening twice a year

biennial – happening once every second year

bibliography – a list of articles or books about a subject

biography – an account of a person's life

bouillon – broth

bullion – uncoined gold or silver

breath – air taken into the lungs

breathe – to inhale and exhale air

calendar – a chart showing the days and months

colander – a strainer

casual – a relaxed, easy manner

causal – relating to a cause

catch – to capture

ketch – a type of boat

cease – to stop

seize – to grab or capture

close – to shut

clothes – apparel; garments

collision – the act of colliding

collusion – a secret plan for wrongdoing

coma – a deep sleep caused by sickness or injury to the brain

comma – a punctuation mark

command – to order

commend – to praise

confidant – a person in whom one can confide

confident – self-assured

conscience – knowledge or sense of right and wrong

conscious – being aware of one's surroundings

contagious – spread by contact (for example, a disease)

contiguous – touching, nearby

cooperation – working together

corporation – a company

costume – special clothing

custom – the habits and usual way of doing things of a people

country – a nation

county – a division of a state

decent – proper

descent – the act of coming down

depraved – morally corrupt

deprived – having something taken away

Easily Confused Words *(continued)*

desert – a dry wasteland
dessert – food served at the end of a meal

device – something built for a specific plan
devise – to invent or scheme

disburse – to pay out
disperse – to scatter

elapse – to pass
lapse – to become void

elicit – to draw out
illicit – unlawful

elusive – hard to catch
illusive – misleading

emerge – to rise out of
immerse – to plunge into

emigrate – to leave one's country to settle
   in another
immigrate – to come into a country to settle

eminent – high in rank
imminent – threatening to occur
   immediately

envelop – to surround
envelope – the cover of a letter

expand – to increase in size
expend – to consume by use

farther – to a greater distance
further – in addition to

fewer – smaller in number
less – not as much

finale – the end
finally – at the end

fiscal – relating to finance
physical – relating to the body

foreword – introduction to a book
forward – toward the front

formally – in a standard or conventional
   manner
formerly – earlier in time

human – a person
humane – kind, benevolent

in – within, inside of
into – motion toward a point inside

ingenious – clever
ingenuous – candid, honest

later – coming afterward
latter – the second of two

lay – to place or put down
lie – to be in a reclined position

least – smallest
lest – for fear that

lend – to give for a time
loan – received to use for a time

THE WRITING TEACHER'S BOOK OF LISTS

lightening – to make less heavy

lightning – a flash of light caused by the discharge of atmospheric electricity

loose – not tight

lose – to be deprived of

massage – body rub

message – a communication

medal – an award

metal – mineral characterized by malleability

moral – ethical, virtuous

morale – strong spirit in time of trouble

of – belong to; from

off – away

past – of a former time

passed – having gone beyond

pastor – a minister

pasture – a grassy field

pedal – a device used to transmit the power of the foot

peddle – to go from place to place selling things

perpetrate – to commit (a crime)

perpetuate – to make enduring

persecute – to harass or annoy

prosecute – to press for punishment of a crime

personal – pertaining to a particular individual

personnel – people employed by a business

picture – a drawing

pitcher – a container for pouring liquids

precede – to go before

proceed – to move onward

pretend – to make believe

portend – to warn; forebode

quiet – still, without noise

quit – to give up

quite – completely

respectfully – in a respectful or considerate manner

respectively – in the order indicated

suppose – assume or imagine

supposed – expected

than – a conjunction that denotes a comparison

then – at that time

thorough – complete

through – going from beginning to end

use – employ

used – secondhand

veracious – truthful

voracious – extremely hungry

Spaceman in the Backyard

DIRECTIONS: Read the following story and circle the correct word from each pair of words. Be careful. The words are easily confused.

The crash in the back yard startled Bobby. He jumped up from the couch where he was reading and hurried to the back window. He rubbed his eyes at the (bizarre, bazaar) sight. Was it an (allusion, illusion)?

Quickly he went outside. The rocket, which was about four feet long, was stuck front first in the ground (beside, besides) the garage. When Bobby bent (close, clothes) to look in the cockpit, he heard a squeaky voice.

"Earthling, I (respectively, respectfully) ask for your (assistance, assistants)."

"What?" said Bobby, astonished.

"Open the hatch," the voice said. "It's stuck."

Bobby pulled on the small door until it popped open. A little man climbed out.

"Thank you," he said.

"What happened?" asked Bobby.

"My craft was struck by (lightening, lightning)," the alien said. "I knew I shouldn't have flown into that thunderstorm, but it was (quit, quite) a light show." He smiled. "May I use your phone?"

"My phone?" asked Bobby.

"How else can I call for a tow-craft?" said the alien.

"Right, sure," said Bobby. (Then, Than) he carried the spaceman inside.

Bobby put the little alien next to the telephone. The alien took a tiny (devise, device) and placed it against the receiver. "Taps into the phone company's computers," he explained. After he was done speaking in a strange language to someone, he put his instrument away. "I'm (confident, confidant) they'll be here soon," he said to Bobby.

He was right. In a few minutes, the tow-craft descended (through, thorough) an opening in the clouds and took hold of the disabled ship.

"Thanks for everything!" the little alien said as he climbed aboard and left.

8

Sound Words

TEACHING SUGGESTIONS

Onomatopoeia refers to the use of words that sound like what they describe. Sound words can effectively add interest and freshness to writing and make it come alive for readers.

When a writer describes *rumbling* thunder, a *crackling* fire, or a *sizzling*, juicy steak, the reader's mind conjures up powerful mental images in which he or she sees as well as hears the action. Students should be made aware of how sound words can enhance their writing.

Activity 1 – Worksheet 8, "Sound Poems"

OBJECTIVE: Students are to write poems that focus on a sound or sounds.

PROCEDURE: Distribute copies of List 8. Give your students a few moments to look over the list, then ask for volunteers to take a sound word and match it with an action. Offer these examples: donkeys bray, wolves howl, old floors creak, and leaves rustle. Have your students name other examples.

For the activity, hand out copies of Worksheet 8 and explain that students are to select a sound or sounds and write a descriptive poem. Completing the worksheet first will help them to organize their ideas. (Depending on the background of your students, you may find it helpful to discuss figures of speech. *See* List 40.) Emphasize that poems may or may not rhyme and may or may not have a specific meter. The focus of the writing should be on the expression, not on the conventions, of poetical form.

You may ask your students to share their poems by reading them to the class, or you may compile them in a book entitled *Sound Poems*.

Activity 2 – A Listening Adventure

OBJECTIVE: Students are to visit a place in which various sounds are apparent and write a description of that place.

PROCEDURE: Distribute copies of List 8 and review the examples of sound words with your students. Explain that, through the effective use of onomatopoeia, writers can create realistic scenes. To write accurately about a place, many authors will go there to experience it firsthand. They carefully observe the area, noting the physical features, and they also listen to the sounds.

For this assignment, ask your students to pick a place in which various sounds are apparent. Offer some examples: the school cafeteria, a park, their backyards, or a school football or basketball game. You might ask students to volunteer some other places. (Emphasize that students should only visit "safe" places.)

Instruct students to visit their chosen sites for at least 15 minutes. They are to listen carefully and take notes of all the sounds they hear. When they return to class, they are to write a descriptive account of the place, detailing all the sounds they heard.

See List 10, "Sensory Words," and List 40, "Figures of Speech."

Sound Words

Sound words, also known as onomatopoeic words, imitate the sounds they describe. Bees *buzz,* telephones *ring,* and cats *meow.* Effective use of sound words can enhance the imagery and realism of writing. Following are examples of sound words.

bang	clip-clop	gong	patter	slurp
bark	clomp	grate	ping	smack
beep	cluck	grind	plop	smash
bong	conk	groan	pop	snort
boo	coo	growl	pow	splash
boom	cough	grunt	puff	squeak
bow-wow	crack	hiss	purr	squeal
bray	crackle	honk	quack	squish
burp	crash	hoot	rap	swish
buzz	creak	howl	rattle	thud
chirp	crinkle	hum	rev	thump
chug	croak	jangle	ring	tick
clack	crunch	jingle	roar	tinkle
clang	cuckoo	knock	rumble	twang
clap	ding-dong	meow	rustle	whack
clash	drip	moan	screech	whiz
clatter	fizz	moo	shriek	whoop
click	flap	neigh	sigh	zip
clink	flop	ooze	sizzle	zoom

Sound Poems

DIRECTIONS: Think of some of the many different kinds of sounds you hear each day. Choose a sound (or sounds), answer the questions below, and write a poem that describes this sound.

1. What sound (or sounds) are the subject of your poem? _____

   _____

   _____

   _____

2. Write a simile that includes this sound. _____

   _____

   _____

   _____

   _____

3. Write a metaphor that includes this sound. _____

   _____

   _____

   _____

   _____

4. Write an example of the sound showing onomatopoeia (if possible). _____

   _____

   _____

   _____

5. Write an example of the sound showing personification (if possible). _____

   _____

   _____

   _____

   _____

9

Compound Words

TEACHING SUGGESTIONS

Compound words are made up of two or more words that have evolved into a single meaning. It is easy to make mistakes with compound words. Frequently, students (and adults) don't recognize compound words or don't know whether to combine, hyphenate, or leave a space between the words that make up the compound. Sometimes dictionaries don't agree either, which only adds to the overall mystery and confusion.

The best thing you can do for your students regarding compound words is to make students aware of these words and encourage them to consult a dictionary or writer's stylebook whenever the slightest doubt arises. Proper use of compound words helps to make writing correct in a mechanical sense, which reflects positively on the author.

Activity 1 – Worksheet 9, "Cookies for the Class Trip"

OBJECTIVE: Students are to identify compound words in a story.

PROCEDURE: Hand out copies of List 9 and discuss compound words with your students. Emphasize that compound words may be closed, hyphenated, or open.

Distribute copies of Worksheet 9. Instruct your students to underline all the compound words they find in the story. You may permit them to use List 9 as a guide in identifying the compound words. After everyone has finished, you may prefer to go over the worksheets orally. Remind your students that they should consult dictionaries or stylebooks whenever they are unsure about the form of a compound word.

ANSWER KEY: Everyone, all out, oatmeal, sidewalk, anything, everybody, afternoon, wild-flowers, sunshine, flowerpot, doorbell, gray-haired, old-fashioned, All right

EXTENSION: Ask your students if, like the character in the story, they have ever done something during which they were nervous. Perhaps they had to sell something, handle an important responsibility, go for a job interview, or give a speech in front of the class. Instruct students to write a descriptive account of this experience. Encourage them to describe what they did as well as how they felt, and, of course, how things turned out. Remind them to pay close attention to any compound words they may use in their writing.

Activity 2 – How Many Can You Find?

OBJECTIVE: Given a list of words, students are to form as many compound words as they can.

PROCEDURE: For this activity, students may work alone, or you may permit them to work in pairs. Begin the activity by distributing copies of List 9 and discussing compound words.

Explain that you will give the class a list of words and that students will be required to form as many compound words from these words as possible. The person or team with the most compound words at the end of the activity wins. You may set a time limit of a class period if you wish or make the activity an overnight assignment. You may allow your students to use dictionaries, as well as List 9, as they work.

Write the following words on the board or an overhead projector for your students to copy:

house	land	way	side
half	rain	flash	light
play	cross	down	man
fall	day	one	walk
back	out	head	some

As an incentive, you should consider offering a prize. You might, for example, add points to the student's last writing assignment. First place might earn 5 points; second place, 3; and third place, 2. You might also put the winners' names on a bulletin board, advertising their accomplishment, and display their list of compound words.

Answers will vary; as long as a word can be substantiated as correct in a dictionary or stylebook, it should be counted.

See List 5, "Hard-to-Spell Words (Intermediate)," and List 6, "Hard-to-Spell Words (Advanced)."

Compound Words

Compound words are words made by combining two or more words. Compound words may be joined, as in *birthday;* connected by a hyphen, as in *drive-in;* or left open, as in *alma mater.* Fortunately, dictionaries are available to lessen the confusion.

able-bodied	basketball	checkmate	dragonfly
above-ground	bathroom	classmate	drive-in
afterthought	battle-axe	classroom	dropout
air conditioner	battleship	clipboard	drugstore
airline	beanbag	close call	dry clean
airmail	birthday	close-up	dust bowl
airplane	birthplace	clothesline	earring
airport	blackboard	cold shoulder	earthquake
all out	blackout	cop-out	everybody
all right	blood pressure	copperhead	everyday
all-American	bloodhound	copyright	eye shadow
all-round	bloodshot	cowboy	eyeball
all-time	bloodstream	cowgirl	eyelid
alma mater	blowup	crosswalk	fairy tale
alongside	blueprint	cupcake	fallout
anchorman	bookcase	custom-made	farmland
anchorwoman	bookkeeper	cutout	filmstrip
anybody	bookmark	dark horse	firehouse
anyhow	box seat	darkroom	fireplace
anymore	boxcar	daydream	fishhook
anyone	breakdown	daytime	flagpole
ashtray	breakneck	dishpan	flashback
back door	broadcast	dogcatcher	flashlight
back talk	brokenhearted	doghouse	floodlight
backbone	brother-in-law	door knob	flowerpot
backyard	bulldog	double talk	folklore
badlands	buttercup	downfall	football
bad-tempered	buttermilk	downpour	forever
barefoot	campfire	downstairs	frogman
baseball	carpool	downtown	frostbite

Compound Words *(continued)*

gentleman	landlord	out-of-bounds	rowboat
goldfish	landslide	outside	runaway
goodbye	lawn mower	overalls	runway
grandfather	leftover	overcoat	rush hour
grasshopper	lifeboat	overlook	safety glass
haircut	lifeguard	overpass	sailboat
half brother	lifeline	pancake	sandpaper
half sister	life-size	paperback	scarecrow
halfway	lightheaded	password	school bus
handcuff	lightweight	payoff	screwball
handlebar	light-year	peanut	seafood
hang-up	lockjaw	peppermint	seagull
hard-boiled	locksmith	pickup	seaside
hardware	lookout	pigtail	self-made
haystack	loudspeaker	pinball	shipwreck
headache	lukewarm	pinch hitter	shoelace
headlight	midnight	pinpoint	shortstop
headline	moonwalk	playmate	showcase
headquarters	motorcycle	playpen	showroom
high rise	newsboy	ponytail	sidewalk
highchair	newscast	popcorn	silverware
highway	newspaper	postcard	skateboard
hilltop	newsprint	postman	skyline
holdup	nightgown	pushover	skyscraper
homemade	nobody	quarterback	slipcover
homework	notebook	quicksand	snowball
horseshoe	oatmeal	railroad	snowdrift
household	old-fashioned	railway	snowfall
housekeeper	outboard	rainbow	snowstorm
infield	outcome	raincoat	softball
jelly bean	outcry	rattlesnake	someone
jellyfish	outfield	redwood	sometime
keyboard	outfit	rip off	spacecraft
keypad	outlaw	riptide	speedboat
landlady	outline	roadside	splashdown

Compound Words *(continued)*

spotlight	thumbtack	uproot	wheelchair
stagehand	time line	upset	whenever
stairway	time-out	uptown	whirlpool
stand-in	timetable	videotape	wholesale
starfish	tiptoe	volleyball	wildcat
stepmother	toenail	washcloth	wildflower
streetcar	toothbrush	washroom	windmill
suitcase	toothpick	watchdog	windpipe
sunbeam	touchdown	watchman	wingspan
sunflower	trade-off	watercolor	without
sweatshirt	tryout	waterfall	woodland
sweetheart	tugboat	waterfront	woodpecker
teacup	turntable	watermelon	wristwatch
teammate	turtleneck	weatherperson	zookeeper
teenager	undercover	weekday	
textbook	undertaker	well-to-do	

Cookies for the Class Trip

DIRECTIONS: Read the following story and circle all of the compound words.

Lori recalled when Mrs. Anderson told the class about the class trip to Walt Disney World. Everyone was excited. Even though it was still a few months away, Mrs. Anderson explained, they had to go all out and raise money for the plane fare as soon as possible. Lori didn't know then that this would mean she would be selling oatmeal cookies.

Standing on the sidewalk before the small, brick house of her neighbor, Mrs. Harris, Lori was nervous. She had never sold anything before. She was afraid of making a mistake and appearing foolish. But everybody had to do his or her part.

Lori took a deep breath and opened the gate. There are better ways to spend a Saturday afternoon, she thought. As she walked toward the porch, she noticed that wildflowers filled the yard. They bloomed in the sunshine and swayed in the soft breeze like gentle waves. They were so pretty that Lori wasn't watching where she was going, and she almost tripped over a flowerpot by the steps.

She groaned at her clumsiness and rang the doorbell. In a moment, an elderly, gray-haired woman with a friendly smile answered.

"Hello, Mrs. Harris," said Lori. "My class is selling tasty, old-fashioned cookies to raise money for our class trip. Would you like to order some?" She offered Mrs. Harris the catalog.

The woman paused a moment as she looked over the selections. "All right, Lori," she said. "Let me see. I can't resist cookies."

10

Sensory Words

TEACHING SUGGESTIONS

Sensory words are those words that appeal to the senses of sight, touch, hearing, smell, and taste. Because they can evoke strong mental images, they are essential to most forms of writing. Sensory words help a reader to vividly imagine the ideas in stories and articles.

Encourage your students to use sensory words in their writing, and point out the effective use of sensory words whenever possible in their reading materials and textbooks. Make your students aware of how authors use sensory words to enhance their stories and articles.

Activity 1 – Worksheet 10, "Smelling the Roses"

OBJECTIVE: Students are to write a description of a special place; they are to use vivid sensory words in their writing.

PROCEDURE: Distribute copies of List 10 and review the sensory words with your students. Explain that these words can help to make writing powerful by providing realistic descriptions.

Hand out copies of Worksheet 10. Instruct your students to complete the worksheet and write a description of a place they know well. Encourage them to use sensory words to sharpen their writing.

Activity 2 – In the Eye of the Beholder

OBJECTIVE: Students are to select a person they know and write a description of this individual.

PROCEDURE: Distribute copies of List 10 and discuss the value of sensory words to writing. For this activity, ask your students to select a person they know well, but who is not in the room. They are to write a description of this person. Encourage students to use sensory words to make this person come alive to readers. (You might like to remind your students to avoid writing negative descriptions of anyone.)

See List 8, "Sound Words."

Sensory Words

Authors rely on sensory words to create strong images. Effective use of sensory words enables readers to *see* the fistfight between the hero and villain, *smell* the dank air of an ancient tomb, *feel* the heat of a raging fire, *hear* the winter wind blow, and *taste* the foods of a grand feast. The following lists of words that refer to the senses of sight, touch, hearing, smell, and taste can help you add realism to your writing.

SIGHT WORDS

angular	dark	homely	shiny
bent	deep	huge	short
big	dim	immense	skinny
billowy	distinct	light	small
black	dull	lithe	smiling
blonde	elegant	little	soaring
blushing	enormous	long	spotless
branching	fancy	low	square
bright	fat	misty	steep
brilliant	filthy	motionless	stern
broad	flat	muddy	stormy
brunette	flickering	murky	straight
bulky	fluffy	narrow	strange
chubby	foggy	obtuse	sunlit
circular	forked	pale	sunny
clean	fuzzy	petite	swooping
cloudy	gigantic	portly	tall
colorful	glamorous	quaint	tapering
colossal	gleaming	radiant	translucent
contoured	glistening	rectangular	ugly
craggy	globular	reddish	unsightly
crinkled	glowing	rippling	unusual
crooked	graceful	rotund	weird
crowded	grotesque	shadowy	wide
crystalline	hazy	shallow	wiry
curved	high	sheer	wispy
cute	hollow	shimmering	wizened

THE WRITING TEACHER'S BOOK OF LISTS

Sensory Words *(continued)*

TOUCH WORDS

breezy	filthy	prickly	solid
bumpy	fluffy	rough	sticky
chilly	frosty	searing	stinging
cold	gooey	shaggy	sweaty
cool	greasy	sharp	tender
cuddly	gritty	silky	tepid
damp	hard	slick	tight
dank	hot	slimy	torrid
dirty	icy	slippery	uneven
downy	loose	slushy	warm
dry	lukewarm	smooth	waxen
dusty	melted	sodden	wet
elastic	plush	soft	wooden

HEARING WORDS

bang	harsh	noisy	snarl
bark	haw	peal	snort
boom	hiss	pop	softly
buzz	hoarse	purr	splash
coo	howl	quietly	squeak
crackling	hushed	raspy	squeal
crash	husky	reverberate	thud
crunch	lapping	rumble	thump
cry	loud	rustle	thunder
deafening	melodious	scream	tinkle
echo	moan	screech	wail
faint	muffled	shriek	whimper
groan	mumble	shrill	whine
growl	murmur	slosh	whisper
gurgle	mutter	snap	whistle

Sensory Words *(continued)*

SMELL WORDS

acrid	delicious	putrid	sour
antiseptic	fragrant	rancid	spicy
bitter	fresh	rich	stale
burning	medicinal	rotten	stinky
choking	musty	salty	strong
clean	pungent	smoky	sweet

TASTE WORDS

acidic	hot	salty	strong
bitter	juicy	savory	sweet
cool	mild	sour	tangy
creamy	nutty	spicy	tart
delicious	peppery	stale	tasteless
gooey	ripe	sticky	tasty

Smelling the Roses

DIRECTIONS: Select a place you know well. Picture it in your mind and try to imagine how this place affects your senses. Answer the questions below; then write a description of this place.

1. What place did you select for your topic? _____

   _____

   _____

   _____

2. Describe this place through the sense of sight. _____

   _____

   _____

   _____

3. Describe this place through the sense of touch. _____

   _____

   _____

   _____

4. Describe this place through the sense of hearing. _____

   _____

   _____

   _____

5. Describe this place through the sense of smell. _____

   _____

   _____

   _____

6. Describe this place through the sense of taste. _____

   _____

   _____

   _____

11

Time Words

TEACHING SUGGESTIONS

Time—we never seem to have enough of it; yet, for most people, it's something that is easy to waste. Indeed, many of us check our watches or clocks several times a day and still manage to be late.

Time is no less important for authors. Time words are essential to the setting of stories and articles. They help clarify transitions, and they allow us to follow the sequence of a story more easily. This is not all they do, though. Imagine trying to characterize a person without using such basic time words as *young* or *old,* or describe an object without using words such as *obsolete, current,* or *new.* Or try to imagine a story evolving without time passing.

Activity 1 – Worksheet 11, "An Accounting of the Day"

OBJECTIVE: Students are to write an account focusing on their actions during a one-day period.

PROCEDURE: Distribute copies of List 11 and discuss the importance of time words to writing. For the activity, hand out copies of Worksheet 11 and instruct your students to write an account of a day—from the time they wake in the morning until they go to sleep at night. Explain that they may use the worksheet to record the day's occurrences. Remind your students to note the way they use time words to clarify their writing.

Activity 2 – Writing an Autobiographical Sketch

OBJECTIVE: Students are to select a part of their lives and write an autobiographical sketch.

PROCEDURE: Distribute copies of List 11 and discuss the importance of time words to writing. Next, review the features of an autobiographical sketch with your students. Explain that it is a brief account of a person's life, written by the subject, and often focuses on an important event, issue, or accomplishment.

Ask your students to think of a time in their lives that they would like to share. Then instruct them to write an autobiographical sketch about this period. Remind them to notice how they use time words to develop their writing.

See List 10, "Sensory Words."

Time Words

Time is one of our most basic concepts. Without the understanding of time passing, tomorrow would never come. It is not surprising, therefore, that time words are fundamental to writing. Time words enable authors to plot stories from beginning to end. They also help to describe settings and characters. Following are examples of words that relate to time.

adolescence	dusk	millennium	semiannual
adulthood	early	minute	short
after	ending	modern	slowly
afternoon	eons	moment	speedy
age	episode	month	sporadic
A.M.	epoch	morning	spring
ancient	era	new	summer
annual	evening	night	sunrise
antiquity	extinct	noon	sunset
bedtime	fall	novel	swift
before	fast	obsolete	tardy
beginning	fleeting	occasional	teenage
biannual	flying	old	twilight
bimonthly	historic	outdated	up-to-date
brief	hour	overdue	week
century	immature	past	winter
childhood	infancy	period	worn-out
clock	instant	P.M.	year
constant	instantaneous	prehistoric	young
continual	interim	prior	youth
crawling	intermittent	prompt	
current	late	punctual	
cyclical	lengthy	quick	
dawn	life span	rapid	
day	long	recent	
daybreak	mature	recur	
daylight	middle age	season	
decade	midnight	second	

An Accounting of the Day

DIRECTIONS: Record the things that happen during your day, then write an account of these occurrences.

Time _____

Occurrence _____

_____

_____

Time _____

Occurrence _____

_____

_____

Time _____

Occurrence _____

_____

_____

Time _____

Occurrence _____

_____

_____

Time _____

Occurrence _____

_____

_____

Time _____

Occurrence _____

_____

_____

LISTS AND ACTIVITIES FOR
Nonfiction Writing

12

Advertising Words

TEACHING SUGGESTIONS

Each day we are bombarded by thousands of advertisements from commercials on TV and radio to displays in windows to classified ads in newspapers and magazines. We see billboards along roadsides and posters on signposts. All of this advertising has a single purpose: to persuade the audience to buy a particular product or service or to form an agreeable opinion about a specific issue. A careful review of advertising reveals that copywriters rely on special words that add power and appeal to their messages. In discussing the various advertising media with your students, be sure to emphasize the words on List 12.

Activity 1 – Worksheet 12, "Being an Ad Writer"

OBJECTIVE: Students are to select a favorite product and write an advertisement for it.

PROCEDURE: A few days in advance of this activity, you might ask your students to bring in examples of advertising copy from newspapers, magazines, and junk mail. Allow some time for the students to exchange the sample ads and discuss them. Emphasize how the ads are designed and written, particularly noting the use of advertising words.

Distribute copies of List 12 and review the words with your students. You will likely find that many of these words appear in the ads your students have examined.

Hand out copies of Worksheet 12. Tell your students to think of a favorite product—a home entertainment center, ten-speed bike, cell phone, ski equipment, or even a comfortable sweater, complete the worksheet, and write an advertisement for this product. They should focus on the product's special features and how consumers would benefit from it.

Activity 2 – Writing a Classified Ad

OBJECTIVE: Students are to write a classified advertisement.

PROCEDURE: Prior to beginning this activity, you should collect examples of classified advertisements in newspapers and magazines. Provide time for sharing these examples of classifieds and note that classified ads are a common and easy method of advertising. Explain that effective classified ads emphasize the features of the items being sold. Just about anything can be sold through classifieds; there are even giveaways!

For this activity, your students are to imagine that they are selling something—their parents' house, a car, bicycle, stereo system, or some other item. They are to write a classified ad. Encourage your students to use words that will influence the readers of their ad to buy.

See List 13, "Business Words," and List 14, "Consumer Words."

Advertising Words

When companies advertise, they try to highlight the best features of their products or services. If you study advertisements carefully, you will see that many of the same words regularly appear in various ads. These words are known to have "pulling power" or audience appeal—they help sell the product or service. Following are several of these words.

best	high (technology, fashion)	reduce
better	hurry	results
brand-new	improved	safety
choose	inexpensive	satisfaction
comfort	introducing	save
courteous	love	security
discover	money	service
don't (wait, delay, miss)	new	simple
easy	now	special
experience	order (today, now)	successful
free	perfect	take
fresh	prize	unique
gift	professional	valuable
grand	proof	warranty
greatest	protect	well-known
guaranteed	proven	
health	quality	

Being an Ad Writer

DIRECTIONS: Think of a favorite product. Complete this worksheet and write an advertisement for this product.

1. What is the name of this product? _____

   _____

2. Name at least three positive features of this product. _____

   _____

   _____

   _____

   _____

   _____

3. What might a customer like about this product? _____

   _____

   _____

   _____

   _____

   _____

4. How would a customer benefit from this product? _____

   _____

   _____

   _____

   _____

   _____

5. What would be a catchy headline to start your advertisement? _____

   _____

   _____

   _____

13

Business Words

TEACHING SUGGESTIONS

Every field of interest has its own vocabulary. Mastery of that vocabulary is a type of initiation into that field. List 13 offers students a glimpse of the vocabulary used by people in business. Definitions are included, as many students may not be familiar with the meaning of some words.

Activity 1 – Worksheet 13, "Starting Your Own Business"

OBJECTIVE: Students are to write an imaginary account of starting a business.

PROCEDURE: Distribute copies of List 13 and briefly review the words with your students. Discuss some of the factors necessary to the success of any business, such as capital, overhead, a salable product or service, location, customers, advertising, pricing, and good service.

Ask your students to think about starting an enterprise of their own. Some examples include providing a grass-cutting service, baby-sitting, running errands for neighbors, and doing odd jobs. Hand out Worksheet 13, and explain that answering the questions will help them to develop their thoughts for writing.

Activity 2 – A Profile of Success

OBJECTIVE: Students are to write a profile of what they consider to be a successful businessperson.

PROCEDURE: Instruct your students to think about the traits a businessperson must have if he or she is to be successful. Some things you might mention include ambition, drive, persistence, knowledge of a product or service, and a willingness to work long hours. Instruct your students to write an article explaining the traits a successful businessperson is likely to have.

See List 12, "Advertising Words," and List 14, "Consumer Words."

Business Words

Following are words that successful businesspeople understand. If they don't, it is unlikely they will stay in business very long!

advertising – a sales presentation directed to potential customers

asset – something of value owned by a company or a person

balance sheet – a periodic statement of a company's assets and liabilities

bankruptcy – the inability of a business or individual to meet financial obligations

capital – any property, assets, or money owned by an individual or business

cash flow – the inflow and outflow of cash

collateral – assets pledged to a lender to secure a loan; assets can be liquidated by the lender to recover the loan in case of a default

competition – rivalry among businesses for the same market

contract – a legal agreement between two or more parties

corporation – a company recognized by laws as a separate entity

default – failure to fulfill an obligation

demand – the need or desire for specific goods or services

discount – a reduction in the price of a product or service

employee – a worker

employer – a person or business who provides work for people

entrepreneur – a person who finances and assumes the risk of new business ventures

finance – relating to money

inventory – the materials, supplies, and goods of a company

job – a position of employment

loan – an amount of money lent, usually to be repaid with interest

market strategy – a plan to achieve sales

need – the lack of something desired

objectives – goals of what a business seeks to accomplish

overhead – the typical operating expenses of a business

partnership – a legal agreement by which two or more people own and operate a business

price – the exchange value of a product or service

production – the conversion of materials into finished products

profit – what remains after the costs of production and marketing have been deducted from income

proprietor – the owner of a business

prospecting – the identification of potential customers

risk – taking a chance that is hoped to result in a gain but may result in a loss

salary – monetary compensation for employees

supply – to provide something that is needed; stock

Starting Your Own Business

DIRECTIONS: Think about the factors responsible for the success of a business. Providing a salable product or service, obtaining capital, advertising, charging a fair price, and providing good service are certainly some considerations. Now think about starting a business of your own. Answer the questions below and write an article describing how you would start a business.

1. What business would you start? _____

   _____

2. What product(s) or service(s) would your business offer? _____

   _____

   _____

   _____

   _____

3. What equipment, if any, would you need? _____

   _____

   _____

   _____

   _____

4. Would you need capital to begin your business? If yes, how much and from whom would

   you obtain it? _____

   _____

   _____

   _____

   _____

5. How would you let potential customers know about your business? _____

   _____

   _____

   _____

   _____

Consumer Words

TEACHING SUGGESTIONS

We are all consumers. An understanding of the words of this list will not only help students become more informed consumers, but will enable them to better comprehend the countless articles and books written for consumers each year.

Activity 1 – Worksheet 14, "Being a Smart Consumer"

OBJECTIVE: Students are to think about buying something they really want, then write an essay describing how they would make sure that the product they buy meets their expectations.

PROCEDURE: Distribute copies of List 14 to your students and review the consumer words. Ask for volunteers to explain how they would go about buying something that is expensive. Would they comparison shop? Would they check prices, features, and warranties? What kinds of questions would they ask salespeople?

Hand out copies of Worksheet 14 and ask your students to imagine that they are about to buy an expensive item they desire. How would they make sure that they were spending their money wisely? Students are to complete the worksheet and then write an essay describing how they would be a smart consumer.

Activity 2 – Writing a Letter to a Company

OBJECTIVE: Students are to write a letter to a company about a product.

PROCEDURE: Ask your students to think of a product or service with which they are either very satisfied or extremely disappointed. You might encourage volunteers to share personal experiences on this subject.

For the assignment, students are to write a letter to the company that made the product or provided the service, offering praise or suggestions for improvement, or simply explaining why they are disappointed. Background Sheet 14 contains examples of the block style and semiblock style for business letters. If your students have the address of the company to which they are writing, they might mail their letters. (If they don't have an actual address, instruct them to use a fictitious address for their letters.)

See List 12, "Advertising Words," and List 13, "Business Words."

Consumer Words

All of us are consumers. Because the audience is so large, numerous articles and books are written for consumers every year. You can be sure that many of the words of the following list also appear in those works.

advertising

arbitration

bait-and-switch

bargain

barter

bonus

budget

buyer

caveat emptor

chain letter

comparison shop

con man (or woman)

contract

credit

credit card

credit rating

customer

debit card

debt

deed

depreciation

discount

estimate

features

fraud

free sample

generic

giveaway

guarantee

installment

interest

interest rate

investment

labeling

layaway

lease

liability

merchandise

mortgage

price

product

purchase

quality

rebate

recall

refund

rent

retail

return

rip-off

sale

sales letter

sales receipt

salesperson

service

service contract

trade

trade-in

warranty

wholesale

Being a Smart Consumer

DIRECTIONS: Think about an expensive product that you really would like to have. It may be a home entertainment center, a computer system, the latest cell phone, a TV, or maybe something even better. What would you do to make sure the product you buy is the best value and meets your expectations? Answer the questions below, then write an essay about how you would be a smart consumer.

1. What product would you buy? _____

   _____

2. Why would you buy this product? _____

   _____

   _____

   _____

3. Would you comparison shop? Why or why not? _____

   _____

   _____

   _____

   _____

4. What questions would you ask the salesperson about this product? _____

   _____

   _____

   _____

   _____

   _____

5. How could you be sure that the product you buy is the best value for your money?

   _____

   _____

   _____

   _____

   _____

Background Sheet 14: Sample Business-Letter Forms

BLOCK STYLE

Your Street
Your City, State, ZIP Code
Date

Name and Title of Addressee
Company Name
Street
City, State, ZIP Code

Dear Mr./Ms. (Name of Person):

Paragraphs are *not* indented in the body.

Sincerely,
(Your Signature)
Your Name

SEMI-BLOCK STYLE

Your Street
Your City, State, ZIP Code
Date

Name and Title of Addressee
Company Name
Street
City, State, ZIP Code

Dear Mr./Ms. (Name of Person):

Paragraphs *are* indented in the body.

Sincerely,
(Your Signature)
Your Name

THE WRITING TEACHER'S BOOK OF LISTS

15

Craft Words

TEACHING SUGGESTIONS

Working with crafts offers enjoyment, relaxation, and an outlet for creativity. Most people experience much satisfaction and pride in producing an item with their own hands. It is likely that many of your students enjoy some type of craft.

Activity 1 – Worksheet 15, "I Made It"

OBJECTIVE: Students are to write a description of something they created or built.

PROCEDURE: Hand out copies of List 15 and review the various crafts with your students. Ask if any of them work with crafts. It is likely that many do. You might ask some of these students to share their experiences with the class.

Distribute copies of Worksheet 15 and ask your students whether they have ever created or built something. It might have been a craft item, a tree house, a snow fort, a model, a puppet, a volcano for a science project—at one time or another they have all made something. Instruct them to write an article about their creation. Answering the questions on the worksheet first will help them organize their thoughts.

Activity 2 – The How and Why of Doing a Craft

OBJECTIVE: Students are to write about a craft they enjoy, how they do the craft, and why they enjoy doing this craft.

PROCEDURE: Ask your students if they do crafts. Many probably do. Ask for volunteers to share with the class any crafts they enjoy and discuss with them why people enjoy crafts.

For this activity, your students are to write an article describing a craft they enjoy. They should include any special skills or materials that are necessary as well as why they enjoy this activity.

See List 22, "Hobby Words," and List 27, "Sports Words."

Craft Words

Crafts offer people a chance to produce something with their own hands, through their own efforts. For many people, crafts are an enjoyable pastime. Others sell their handiwork and turn their skills into a successful business. In either case, few things are as satisfying as those we create ourselves. Following are common crafts.

basketry	engraving	pottery making
batik	fabric painting	printmaking
calligraphy	flower arranging	quilting
candle making	jewelry making	rug hooking
candy making	knitting	sculpting
carpentry	lace making	sewing
ceramics	leather working	silk screening
crocheting	macramé	stained glass
cross stitching	metal working	stenciling
doll making	model building	stone carving
dollhouse building	needlepoint	tie-dyeing
egg decorating	origami	toy making
embroidery	painting	weaving
enameling	papier-mâché	woodworking

I Made It

DIRECTIONS: Think of something you have made. It might be a craft item, or something else. Answer the questions below and then write an article about what you made.

1. What did you make? _____
   _____

2. What was it for? _____
   _____
   _____
   _____

3. What materials did you use? _____
   _____
   _____
   _____
   _____

4. What special skills and tools did you use? _____
   _____
   _____
   _____
   _____

5. What steps did you take in producing your creation? _____
   _____
   _____
   _____
   _____

6. What eventually happened to your creation? _____
   _____
   _____
   _____

16

Ecology Words

TEACHING SUGGESTIONS

As we become more aware of the dynamic relationships among the organisms of our world, as well as their relationships to their environment, we realize how complex the webs of life are. The following list by no means includes all the words and concepts of ecology, but it does contain the basics and provides a good starting point. Emphasize to your students that these words are used by authors who write about nature and its wondrous diversity.

Activity 1 – Worksheet 16, "A Speech About the Environment"

OBJECTIVE: Students are to select a topic about ecology and write and present a speech.

PROCEDURE: Hand out copies of List 16 and review the words with your students. Note that ecology is the study of the interactions and relationships between organisms and their environment. For the activity, instruct your students to pick a topic from the words on List 16 or to choose any other topic of their own regarding ecology. They are to research their topics, write a speech, and give their speech to the class.

To help your students focus their ideas, distribute copies of Worksheet 16. Explain that completing the worksheet will help them organize their speeches. Encourage students to use the library and on-line sources to develop their material with pertinent facts and details.

Activity 2 – Changing Places

OBJECTIVE: Students are to imagine that they are a plant or animal; they are to write a description of their environment from this viewpoint.

PROCEDURE: Ask your students to pretend that they are a plant or an animal that lives in their home, yard, or surrounding area. If they were this organism, how would they see their environment?

For example, to a squirrel, an oak tree appears to be much larger than it does to us; yet a squirrel is entirely at ease in that tree. We might consider the tree to be little more than a decoration for the yard, but to the squirrel it provides safety, a home, and food (acorns). Emphasize that when we change points of view, we also change perceptions. For the assignment, students are to put themselves in the place of a plant or an animal and write about their environment from this new point of view.

See List 26, "Science Words."

Ecology Words

Ecology—the study of living things and their relationships to each other and the environment—is as broad as the world itself. The following list focuses on some of the most important words and concepts in ecology.

acid rain	ecosystem	mineral
adaptation	endangered species	mountain
algae	energy	natural resources
amphibians	environment	natural selection
animals	erosion	nutrients
atmosphere	evaporation	oceans
bacteria	evergreen	omnivore
balance of nature	evolution	organic
biology	extinct	organism
biomes	fauna	oxygen
birds	fertile	parasite
bog	fish	peat
carbon dioxide	flora	photosynthesis
carnivore	food web	plants
cell	forest	pollution
chlorophyll	grassland	pond
climate	greenhouse effect	population
cold-blooded	habitat	prairie
community	host	precipitation
competition	humus	predator
coniferous	inorganic	prey
conservation	insects	producer
consumer	instinct	rain forest
cycle	interaction	rainfall
decay	invertebrates	reproduction
deciduous	lakes	reptiles
decomposers	life cycle	respiration
decomposition	mammals	rivers
desert	marine life	savanna
earth	microorganisms	scavenger

Ecology Words *(continued)*

smog	territoriality	warm-blooded
soil	tides	water table
species	trees	water vapor
streams	tropics	watershed
succession	tundra	weather
symbiosis	vegetation	wetlands
taiga	vertebrates	zoology

A Speech About the Environment

DIRECTIONS: Select a topic in ecology. Answer the following questions, and then write a speech about your topic. (Be sure to research thoroughly.) Give your speech to the class.

1. What is your topic? _____

   _____

2. Why did you choose this topic? _____

   _____

   _____

   _____

   _____

3. Why is this topic important? _____

   _____

   _____

   _____

   _____

   _____

4. Can the understanding of your topic help improve the environment? If yes, how? If no,

   why not? _____

   _____

   _____

   _____

   _____

5. Does your topic have significance for the future? If yes, in what way? _____

   _____

   _____

   _____

Education Words

TEACHING SUGGESTIONS

Most students find it easier to write about topics with which they have direct experience. School surely is one such topic. The words of this list will provide students with the vocabulary needed to write about school-related topics and issues.

Activity 1 – Worksheet 17, "What's Right and Wrong with My School"

OBJECTIVE: Students are to write an essay describing what they feel is right and wrong with their school.

PROCEDURE: Hand out copies of List 17 and review the words with your students. Generate a discussion about your school, encouraging students to share their feelings about its good points as well as areas in which they feel it can be improved. Explain that their assignment is to write an essay about the positive and negative aspects of their school.

Distribute copies of Worksheet 17 and note that completing the worksheet will help them to clarify their ideas for their essays. After your students have completed the activity, you might display their essays so that other students may read the opinions of their classmates.

EXTENSION: Divide your students into groups of two or three. Instruct them to design and make a report card in which they grade their school. Suggest that they use construction paper or oak tag for their "school" report cards.

Activity 2 – If I Were a Teacher

OBJECTIVE: Students are to imagine that they are teachers and write about how they would conduct their class.

PROCEDURE: Distribute copies of List 17 and review the words with your students. Begin the activity by explaining that every teacher has individual instructional methods. Ask students to think about the methods their teachers use that they, as students, like best. Some students may prefer independent study, others may like to listen to lectures, and still others may prefer learning by way of discussion.

Now ask your students to imagine that they are teachers. What subject would they teach? How would they set up and conduct their class? What rules would they insist be followed? Instruct your students to write about their imaginary experience as teachers.

See List 19, "Words of Government and Politics."

Education Words

Not too long ago, Americans attended class in one-room schoolhouses. Today, it is not uncommon for a student to go to preschool, elementary school, middle school, high school, college, and graduate school. Following are words that have become important parts of the American educational establishment.

ability	example	objective
achievement	fail	pass
activity	feedback	peer
administrator	goal	percentage
answer	grade	percentile
assessment	graduation	preschool
assignment	group	principal
basics	guidance counselor	problem solving
behavior	high school	professor
book	higher education	proficiency
children	homework	program
class	honor roll	promotion
classroom	illiteracy	pupil
college	instruction	question
communication	instructor	reading
content	IQ (intelligence quotient)	remediation
course	junior high school	research
creativity	knowledge	resources
curriculum	language arts	responsibility
degree	learning	retention
dialogue	lesson	schedule
diploma	library	school
discipline	literacy	science
dropout	mastery	score
elementary school	mathematics	social studies
ESL (English as a second language)	mentor	special education
evaluation	middle school	spelling
	motivation	sports

Education Words *(continued)*

standardized

student

study

subject matter

teacher

test

text

theory

thinking

university

vice principal

vocational

writing

THE WRITING TEACHER'S BOOK OF LISTS

What's Right and Wrong with My School

DIRECTIONS: Everything in life has good and bad points. School is no exception. Complete this worksheet and write an essay entitled "What's Right and Wrong with My School."

1. List at least three things that are "right" with your school. _____

   _____

   _____

   _____

   _____

   _____

   _____

   _____

2. List at least three things that are "wrong" with your school. _____

   _____

   _____

   _____

   _____

   _____

   _____

   _____

3. How can the "wrongs" be improved? _____

   _____

   _____

   _____

   _____

   _____

   _____

   _____

18

Food Words

TEACHING SUGGESTIONS

Countless articles and books about food are written each year. These works range from the latest recipes for exotic delicacies to articles warning about pesticide residue on our vegetables. List 18 provides the basics that will help your students write about food with delicious effectiveness.

Activity 1 – Worksheet 18, "It's Time to Feast"

OBJECTIVE: Students are to write a descriptive account about a feast of their favorite foods.

PROCEDURE: Begin the activity by distributing copies of List 18 and reviewing the words with your students. Ask volunteers to describe their favorite foods. For the assignment, students are to imagine that they are having a feast—a full-course dinner—of their favorite foods and write a descriptive account of the meal.

Hand out copies of Worksheet 18. Note that completing the worksheet will help students organize and develop their ideas for writing.

Activity 2 – Making a Meal Plan

OBJECTIVES: Students are to design a week-long meal plan; they are to write a description of their meal plan.

PROCEDURE: Distribute copies of List 18 and review the words with your students. Encourage a discussion of the importance of good nutrition and a balanced diet. You might ask your students to mention examples of healthy foods and so-called junk foods. You might also briefly discuss the five basic food groups:

1. The bread, cereal, rice, and pasta group
2. The vegetable group
3. The fruit group

4. The meat, fish, poultry, eggs, dry beans, and nut group

5. The milk, yogurt, and cheese group

For this activity, explain that students are to design a one-week meal plan. They are to include breakfast, lunch, and dinner, as well as snacks. An effective way to complete this part of the assignment is to develop the meal plan in the form of a chart. Students will find much of the information they will need from List 18; however, encourage them to use reference materials. Depending on how detailed you want this activity to be, it may be advisable to provide time for students to work on it over a few periods.

After your students have completed their charts, they are to write a summary of their meal plans. On completion of the activity, you may wish to display the charts and summaries.

See List 20, "Health Words," and List 26, "Science Words."

Food Words

Eating is often described as one of the great joys in life. Whereas our ancient ancestors were limited to a diet of nuts, roots, wild vegetables, and coarse meat, we can pick from a variety of dishes that entice our taste buds. Many authors earn their bread by writing about food.

additive	culinary	kosher	pretzel
appetite	cutlery	leftover	protein
appetizer	dessert	lunch	pudding
bagel	diet	margarine	quiche
bake	digestion	mayonnaise	recipe
biscuit	dinner	meat	salad
boil	dish	meatball	salt
bread	egg	milk	sandwich
breakfast	fat	mineral	sauce
broil	fiber	mousse	seed
brunch	fish	mustard	shellfish
butter	flour	napkin	snack
cake	fork	nut	soup
calorie	French fries	omelet	spaghetti
candy	fruit	pancake	spoon
carbohydrate	fry	pasta	stew
cellulose	goulash	pastry	stuffing
cereal	gourmet	peanut	sugar
cheese	grain	pepper	taco
chef	granola	pickle	toast
cholesterol	gravy	pie	transfat
chow	herb	pizza	TV dinner
condiment	honey	poach	vegetable
cook	ice cream	popcorn	venison
cookie	junk food	potato	vitamin
cottage cheese	ketchup (catsup)	potato chip	water
cracker	kitchen	poultry	yogurt
cuisine	knife	preservative	

THE WRITING TEACHER'S BOOK OF LISTS

It's Time to Feast

DIRECTIONS: Think of your favorite foods. If you could plan your favorite meal, what would you have? Complete this worksheet and then write about your favorite foods and the best meal of your life.

Appetizers: _____

_____

_____

Soups: _____

_____

_____

Main Courses: _____

_____

_____

_____

Desserts: _____

_____

_____

Beverages: _____

_____

_____

With whom would you share your feast? Why? _____

_____

_____

_____

_____

19

Words of Government and Politics

TEACHING SUGGESTIONS

While politicians love to spin catchy phrases to explain their latest proposals, government agencies regularly invent new words and terminology to describe their programs and policies. There never seems to be a shortage of governmental or political gobbledygook. The words of List 19 will *not* be found on any one government document or in any one political platform, but they constitute a basic vocabulary for anyone who wants to write about the American political scene.

Activity 1 – Worksheet 19, "Personal Policies"

OBJECTIVE: Students are to write an article describing the types of changes they would make in their town if they were mayor.

PROCEDURE: Hand out copies of List 19 and review the words with your students. Discuss briefly the role that government and politics play in a democratic society.

To help your students organize their thoughts for this activity, distribute copies of Worksheet 19. Instruct students to assume that they are the mayor of their town and that they have the power to change the way the town is run. What changes would they make? Why? After completing the worksheet, students are to write an article describing the changes they would make in their town.

Activity 2 – A Student Bill of Rights

OBJECTIVE: Students are to write a Student Bill of Rights.

PROCEDURE: Discuss the Bill of Rights with your students. (You might find it helpful to work with their social studies teacher on this one.) Ask your students to consider what rights students should have, then instruct them to write a Student Bill of Rights.

Depending on your students, you may allow them to work in small groups. At the end of the assignment you might combine the best features of the writings and compile a class Student Bill of Rights.

EXTENSION: Carry this activity a step further and have the groups write a School Constitution that outlines the roles of administrators, teachers, and students in your school. It would be helpful to briefly review the U.S. Constitution before starting this activity.

See List 17, "Education Words."

Words of Government and Politics

Government employees and politicians are two of the greatest inventors of words and phrases. New ideas, changes in policies, and fresh regulations require explanations and directions. The following list contains important words relating to government and politics.

accountability	convention	law
administration	coordination	leadership
agency	corruption	Left (the)
alien	council	legislation
alliance	county	liberal
amendments	court	lobby
appointee	decision making	management
arms control	Declaration of Independence	mayor
Assembly	delegate	media
assistance	Democrat	mediation
authorize	document	Medicaid
ballot	election	Medicare
benefits	ethics	nation
Bill of Rights	evaluation	objectives
budget	executive	ombudsman
bureaucracy	federal	organization
cabinet	filibuster	PAC (political action
campaign	foreign policy	committee)
caucus	goals	patriotism
centralization	governor	patronage
citizen	grants	petition
city	Hawks	pluralism
civil rights	House of Representatives	policy
civil service	income tax	political party
committee	institution	poll
compromise	interest groups	pragmatism
Congress	international	president
Congressman/woman	judiciary	primary
conservative	jury	program
Constitution	Justice	propaganda

Words of Government and Politics *(continued)*

public	Right (the)	Supreme Court
public advocate	rights	survey
public opinion	Senate	tax
quotas	senator	town
reactionary	Social Security	United Nations
red tape	sound bite	veto
representative	spin master	vote
Republican	staff	
revolution	state	

Personal Policies

DIRECTIONS: Imagine that you have just been appointed mayor of your town. You have the authority to change the way the town is run. What changes would you make? Complete this worksheet and write an article about the changes you would make in your town. Be sure to include valid reasons.

1. What policy, rule, or law would you change first? Why? _____

_____

_____

_____

_____

_____

_____

2. What other policies, rules, or laws would you change? Why? _____

_____

_____

_____

_____

_____

_____

_____

3. How would these changes improve your town? _____

_____

_____

_____

_____

_____

_____

20

Health Words

TEACHING SUGGESTIONS

Health is a topic that is often ignored by students. After all, most young people feel invincible. As our population ages and many people become more health conscious, the words of List 20 increase in significance. Many of these words can be found in the countless health articles and books that are published each year.

Activity 1 – Worksheet 20, "A Subject of Health"

OBJECTIVE: Students are to write an article on a topic in health.

PROCEDURE: Distribute copies of List 20 to your students. Briefly review the words, then ask them to volunteer what they feel are significant health problems or issues. Suggestions might include AIDS (Acquired Immune Deficiency Syndrome), cancer, heart disease, drug abuse, alcoholism, smoking, lack of proper nutrition, and insufficient exercise. You might list these topics on the board or an overhead projector. For the assignment, students are to write an article on a health topic of their choice.

Distribute copies of Worksheet 20, which will help students organize their ideas for writing. Encourage them to conduct research if necessary and suggest that for current topics they search on-line sources.

Activity 2 – "How to Get Along with People"

OBJECTIVE: Students are to write an essay on how to get along with others.

PROCEDURE: Briefly discuss with your students the topic that emotional health can be as important as physical health. One of the aspects of emotional health is enjoying good personal relationships with others. The development of positive relationships depends on the ability to get along with other people. For this assignment, students are to write an essay entitled "How to Get Along with People."

To help your students clarify their thoughts, suggest that they compose a simple listing of ideas. On one side of a sheet of paper, they should list four or five behaviors that they like in some of the people they know. On the other side of the sheet, they should list four or five behaviors that they do not like. From this they should be able to develop their essays. Remind students to include specific details and examples to support their ideas.

See List 18, "Food Words," and List 26, "Science Words."

Health Words

Good health is truly a blessing, yet most of us fail to appreciate its value until it is lost. Following are words associated with health.

accident	diagnosis	nurse
aging	dialysis	nutrition
AIDS (Acquired Immune Deficiency Syndrome)	diet	obesity
	digestion	organ transplants
alcoholism	disability	painkillers
allergies	disease	penicillin
anemia	disorder	pharmacy
antibiotic	drug abuse	phobia
antihistamine	epidemic	physician
anxiety	exercise	pneumonia
appendicitis	fatigue	poisoning
arthritis	first aid	prognosis
aspirin	headache	respiration
attitude	heart disease	seizure
backache	heredity	senility
bacteria	HIV	sleep
biofeedback	hyperactivity	sleep disorder
biopsy	hypothermia	smoking
bioterrorism	immune system	stress
bronchitis	immunization	stroke
cancer	infection	substance abuse
checkup	influenza (the flu)	surgeon
cholesterol	insomnia	surgery
circulation	insulin	tumor
colds	kidney disease	ulcer
coma	leukemia	vaccination
cough	malignancy	vaccine
deafness	medicine	virus
depression	metabolism	weight
dermis	migraine	wound
diabetes	nausea	X ray

A Subject of Health

DIRECTIONS: Select a topic in health and write an article about it. Completing this worksheet first will help you focus your efforts. Consult reference books as well as on-line sources for your research.

1. What health topic have you selected to write about? _____

   _____

   _____

2. Why is this topic important to you? _____

   _____

   _____

   _____

   _____

   _____

   _____

3. Write at least three questions about your topic that you hope to answer during the course

   of your research: _____

   _____

   _____

   _____

   _____

   _____

   _____

   _____

   _____

   _____

   _____

21

History Words

TEACHING SUGGESTIONS

It is often said that those who don't understand the past will repeat it. The words of the following list will not only help your students to understand history, but also enhance their ability to write about it.

Activity 1 – Worksheet 21, "I Was There"

OBJECTIVE: Students are to imagine they lived in the past and witnessed a historical event; they are to write an imaginary journal entry describing their experience.

PROCEDURE: Distribute copies of List 21 and review the words with your students. For this activity, ask your students to imagine that they are living in the past during a time of historical significance. Offer some examples such as the assassination of Julius Caesar, Columbus's discovery of the New World, the Pilgrims' first Thanksgiving, or the Battle of Gettysburg. Students are to assume they were present at the time of the event and record what happened in a journal. You might find it necessary to explain that a journal contains personal writing in which an individual can record events, ideas, and opinions.

To help your students organize their thoughts, hand out copies of Worksheet 21. Remind students that they will require accurate information to write about their event effectively. While some students may consult their history texts for details about events, others may need to consult additional sources.

Activity 2 – I Wish I Lived Back Then

OBJECTIVE: Students are to imagine that they could have lived in another historical period; they are to write about what their lives would have been like.

PROCEDURE: Distribute copies of List 21 and briefly review the words with your students. If they could choose a time of the past in which to live, which period would they choose? Explain that for the assignment, they are to imagine that they lived during that time and write a description of how their lives would have been.

Encourage students to describe how each day would be. What would they like best about their lives in this former time? What would they like least? How would their lives be similar to their lives today? How would they be different? Why would they like to live in the period they chose?

See List 19, "Words of Government and Politics."

History Words

It is difficult to understand the present without understanding the past. The following words shed some light on events that have resulted in how we live today.

abolish	candidate	debate
abolitionist	capitalism	debt
absolute monarchy	capitol	declaration
alien	carpetbagger	Declaration of Independence
alliance	caucus	defense
allies	census	delegate
amendment	charter	democracy
American Revolution	checks and balances	Democrat
amnesty	citizen	desegregation
ancient	civil rights	dictatorship
annex	Civil War	diplomacy
apartheid	civilization	disarmament
archaeology	cold war	discrimination
aristocracy	colonization	dissent
armada	colony	divine right
armistice	commerce	draft
artifact	commonwealth	dynasty
assembly	communism	economy
autocracy	compromise	election
balance of power	Confederacy	emancipation
barbarian	Congress	embargo
barter	conquer	emigration
battle	conservative	emperor
Bill of Rights	Constitution	empire
bloc	convention	equality
blockade	council	ethnic group
boundary	country	exile
boycott	culture	export
bureaucracy	currency	fascism
cabinet	customs	federal
campaign	czar	

History Words *(continued)*

Federal Reserve
Federalist
filibuster
fleet
foreign policy
Free World
freedom
frontier
goods
government
governor
grange
Great Depression
history
homestead
illiteracy
immigrant
immigration
impeach
imperialism
import
inaugurate
indenture
independence
inflation
integration
invasion
Iron Curtain
isolationism
judicial
jury
labor
laissez-faire
Latin America
law

legal
legislature
liberal
loyalist
majority
mandate
Manifest Destiny
manufacture
martial law
mercantilism
merchant
middle class
Middle East
migrant
militia
minority
Minutemen
missionary
moderate
monarchy
monotheism
Monroe Doctrine
mother country
muckraker
nationalism
Native American
NATO (North Atlantic
    Treaty Organization)
Nazism
negotiation
neutrality
New Deal
New World
nobility
Northwest Passage

occupied
oppression
Orient
pacifist
Parliament
patriotism
peasant
peon
per capita
persecution
petition
plantation
platform
policy
political party
politics
polytheism
postwar
poverty
prehistoric
prejudice
president
primary
primary source
prime minister
proclamation
progressive
Prohibition
propaganda
prospector
protectorate
protest
Protestant
province
provision

History Words *(continued)*

public domain

public opinion

Puritan

radical

ratify

raw material

rebellion

recession

reconstruction

referendum

reform

Reformation

refugee

regulation

religion

repeal

representative

republic

Republican

reservation

resolution

retreat

revenue

revolt

Revolution

revolution

Revolutionary War

royalist

sabotage

sanction

scandal

secede

secession

secondary source

segregation

Senate

senator

settlement

sharecropper

siege

slavery

smuggling

Social Security

socialism

socialist

sovereignty

stock market

strategy

surplus

surrender

sweatshop

tariff

taxation

territory

terrorism

tolerance

totalitarian

trade

tradition

traitor

transcontinental

treason

treaty

truce

tyranny

tyrant

UN (United Nations)

unconstitutional

underdeveloped

veto

welfare

wilderness

I Was There

DIRECTIONS: Imagine that you witnessed a historical event. Complete the worksheet and write an imaginary journal entry of that event.

1. What event did you witness? _____

_____

2. When and where did the event take place? _____

_____

_____

3. Who was present? _____

_____

_____

_____

4. Why did the event happen? _____

_____

_____

_____

5. Describe what happened. _____

_____

_____

_____

_____

6. Describe the historical significance of the event. _____

_____

_____

_____

_____

_____

Hobby Words

TEACHING SUGGESTIONS

Everyone needs a hobby, and most people have at least one. It is likely that your students enjoy a variety of different hobbies.

Activity 1 – Worksheet 22, "My Hobby"

OBJECTIVE: Students are to write an article about a hobby.

PROCEDURE: Distribute copies of List 22 and review the words with your students. Conduct a discussion about hobbies.

To begin the assignment, hand out copies of Worksheet 22 and explain that students are to complete the worksheet, then write an article about their hobby. Remind them to include why they like this hobby and what it entails.

Activity 2 – Writing about After-School Hobbies

OBJECTIVE: Students are to write an essay entitled "Why Our School Should (or Should Not) Offer After-School Hobbies."

PROCEDURE: Explain that many schools run after-school activities or hobbies for their students. If your school does, instruct your students to write an essay on why they feel this program is or is not worthwhile. Encourage them to support their ideas with details and examples. If your school does not have an activities program, or if your students would prefer activities that are not offered, they should write their essays explaining their feelings from these perspectives.

EXTENSION: If your school doesn't have an activities program and students are in favor of one, you might pass their essays along to the appropriate administrators to see whether a program can be established. This would provide students with a strong incentive to develop their ideas and write clearly.

See List 15, "Craft Words," and List 27, "Sports Words."

Hobby Words

Hobbies offer people a chance for fun, relaxation, and a feeling of accomplishment. They can be a pleasant escape from the rigors and stresses of the modern world. Following is a list of popular hobbies.

antique collecting	drama	radio-controlled vehicles
arts and crafts	fishing	reading
astronomy	flower arranging	restorations
baking	flower collecting	rock collecting
bird watching	gardening	scrapbooks
boating	hiking	sewing
book collecting	magic	shell collecting
butterfly collecting	miniatures	singing
camping	model building	sketching
candy making	music	sports
card collecting	nature study	stamp collecting
chess	painting	stenciling
coin collecting	pets	travel
cooking	photography	volunteering
dancing	puppetry	writing
doll collecting	puzzles	

My Hobby

DIRECTIONS: Think about your hobbies. Select one, complete this worksheet, and then write a descriptive article about your hobby.

1. My hobby is: _____

_____

2. Why do you like this hobby? _____

_____

_____

_____

_____

_____

3. Describe any special materials necessary for your hobby. _____

_____

_____

_____

_____

_____

_____

4. How does a person participate in your hobby? _____

_____

_____

_____

_____

_____

_____

23

Math Words

TEACHING SUGGESTIONS

In the past, when most people thought of mathematics, they thought only of numbers and formulas. Today, however, people, especially teachers, have come to realize that writing is an essential part of learning math. Along with being able to express mathematical ideas clearly, students are often required to write explanations of the solutions to problems. The words of List 23 offer a solid foundation for writing about mathematics.

Activity 1 – Worksheet 23, "A Time for Math"

OBJECTIVE: Students are to write an essay explaining the importance of mathematics.

PROCEDURE: Distribute copies of List 23 and review the math words with your students. Ask how many of them like math. Certainly some hands will go up. Now ask how many (even if they don't like math) realize mathematics is an important subject. Most, if not all, hands should rise.

Begin a brief discussion of the ways mathematics is important. Some ideas you might focus on include: math and finance, math and science and technology, and math and commerce. You might mention that lacking basic knowledge in math can make such routine tasks as balancing a checkbook challenging.

To help your students focus their ideas for writing, hand out copies of Worksheet 23. Instruct your students to complete the worksheet, then write their essays. Remind them to support their ideas with details.

Activity 2 – When Two and Two Do Not Equal Four

OBJECTIVE: Students are to write an article explaining how numbers can be written in a base other than base 10.

PROCEDURE: This can be a challenging activity, especially for students who do not have experience with bases, and you might find it worthwhile to consult their math teacher before beginning this assignment. To start the activity, distribute copies of List 23 and briefly review the words with your students. Explain that the base of any number system refers to the number of different symbols used. We use the Arabic system, which is a base 10 system because ten symbols are used in writing the numbers: 0, 1, 2, 3, 4, 5, 6, 7, 8, 9. Number systems can be based on any amount of symbols, however. The binary system, which is base 2, for example, has only two digits, 0 and 1.

For this activity, your students are to select a number system other than base 10 and write an article describing the number system. Encourage them to offer some examples of how a person would work with this number system. While information about other number systems may be found in some math textbooks, it is likely that your students will need to consult reference books.

See List 26, "Science Words."

Math Words

When most people think about math, they think about numbers. The field of mathematics, however, also contains an extensive vocabulary. A thorough understanding of this vocabulary is necessary when a person discusses or writes about math. Following are some of the most common words of mathematics.

absolute value	computation	fewer
addition	coordinate plane	figure
algebra	coordinate	fractal
amount	count	frequency
angle	cross product	function
arithmetic	cube	geometry
array	data	graph
associative property	decimal point	greater than
average	degree	greatest
axiom	denominator	grid
bar graph	diagonal	group
base	diameter	grouping
between	difference	half
billion	digit	horizontal
calculate	distance	hundred
calculus	distributive property	improper fraction
center	divide	increase
change	divisible	inequality
circle	division	infinite
circle graph	divisor	integer
circumference	domain	interest
combine	empty set	interpret
common denominator	equal	intersect
common factor	equation	inverse
common multiple	estimate	irrational number
commutative property	even number	kite
compare	exponent	less
compass	expression	less than
composite number	factor	line

line graph	pattern	rename
many	percent	rhombus
mathematics	perfect square	rotation
mean	perimeter	rounding
measure	perpendicular	segment
median	pi	semicircle
member	pictograph	sequence
midpoint	pie graph	set
million	place holder	sign
minimum	place value	similar
minus	plane	simplest form
mixed number	plus	simplify
mode	polygon	slope
model	positive	solution
more	prime factor	solve
most	principle	space
multiple	prism	square
multiplication	probability	square number
multiply	problem	statistics
natural number	product	subset
negative	proper fraction	subtract
number	proportion	sum
number line	pyramid	surface area
number sentence	quadrant	symbol
numeral	quadrilateral	symmetric
numerator	quotient	table
odd number	radius	theorem
operation	range	thousand
order of operations	ratio	times
ordinal number	ray	total
origin	reciprocal	transformation
pair	rectangle	trapezoid
parallel	reflection	triangle
parallelogram	regroup	trigonometry
parentheses	remainder	trillion

Math Words *(continued)*

unequal	value	whole number
union	vertex	*x*-axis
unit	vertical	*y*-axis
unknown	volume	zero

A Time for Math

DIRECTIONS: Complete the worksheet and write an essay on the ways mathematics is important to our lives.

1. List some examples of how math is important in the use and exchange of money.

   _____

   _____

   _____

   _____

   _____

2. List some examples of how math is important to business. _____

   _____

   _____

   _____

   _____

   _____

3. List some examples of how math is important to science and technology. _____

   _____

   _____

   _____

   _____

   _____

4. List some examples of how math is important to you and your family. _____

   _____

   _____

   _____

   _____

   _____

   _____

Music Words

TEACHING SUGGESTIONS

From its earliest origins in simple chants and rhythmic drumming, music has evolved to become a major element of modern life. Music can inspire, uplift, or bring tears to our eyes. It can etch itself into our minds and hearts and evoke powerful emotions and memories. It also provides an excellent writing topic for students.

Activity 1 – Worksheet 24, "My Kind of Music"

OBJECTIVE: Students are to write an essay describing the type of music they prefer.

PROCEDURE: Distribute copies of List 24 and review the music words with your students, noting that this list contains only some of the most common words in the field of music. Discuss types of music that are popular among your students, highlighting how they are different from one another. Examples might include rock and roll, country, rap, jazz, or maybe even classical. It is likely your students will name others.

Hand out copies of Worksheet 24. Note that answering the questions on the worksheet will help students to organize their thoughts for writing. Remind them to support their ideas with specific details.

Activity 2 – Making Music

OBJECTIVE: Students are to write the lyrics for a song of their own composition.

PROCEDURE: You may prefer to have your students work in pairs or groups of three for this activity. When forming the groups, try to ensure that at least one of the members of each group has some musical background. Such background can be helpful to the group's efforts at completing the activity.

To begin the activity, instruct your students to pick a favorite type of music. Explain that they are to write lyrics for a song of their own creation. (After all, lyricists are writers.) While students should focus on the lyrics, encourage them to also create a melody if possible.

When your students have finished, ask for volunteers to perform their songs for the class. While this may be little more than reciting lyrics for some groups, others will surprise you with their enthusiasm and talent.

See List 22, "Hobby Words."

Music Words

The words of the list below are likely to be familiar to most people who enjoy music. Although the list is limited to common music words, it still provides a glimpse of how broad and extensive the subject of music is.

accompanist	doo-wop	music video
album	duet	mute
allegro	duo	neoclassical
alternative	ensemble	note
aria	flat	octave
arranger	folk	opera
audition	forte	orchestra
ballad	gospel	percussion
band	group	performance
bar	harmony	pitch
bass	heavy metal	pop
baton	hip-hop	practice
beat	hymn	quartet
chord	impromptu	rap
choreographer	instrument	recital
choreography	instrumental	record
chorus	jam session	recording
classical	jazz	refrain
clef	keyboard	rehearse
compact disc (CD)	keys	rhythm and blues (R&B)
composer	lyric	rock and roll
composition	lyricist	scale
concert	maestro	score
concerto	marching band	sharp
conductor	measure	sheet music
contemporary	melody	signature
country	metronome	single
disc jockey (DJ)	microphone	solo
diva	movement	soloist

Music Words *(continued)*

soprano staff strings superstar symphony

talent tape tape deck tempo time

Tin Pan Alley trio veejay wind

My Kind of Music

DIRECTIONS: Think of different forms of music, such as rock and roll, country, jazz, and rap. Answer the questions and write an essay describing your favorite type of music.

1. What is your favorite type of music? _____
   _____

2. Describe this music. _____
   _____
   _____
   _____
   _____
   _____
   _____

3. How is it different from other forms of music? _____
   _____
   _____
   _____
   _____
   _____
   _____
   _____
   _____

4. Why do you prefer this type of music over others? (Be specific.) _____
   _____
   _____
   _____
   _____
   _____
   _____
   _____

Words of Newspapers and Magazines

TEACHING SUGGESTIONS

Newspapers and magazines (both print and on-line) offer a variety of features and articles. They are significant sources of information. While some publications are designed for a specific audience, others remain general in focus and appeal.

Most newspapers and magazine articles are written with short, clear sentences. Articles may rely on research and interviews or may be based on observation or firsthand experience.

Virtually all general interest magazine articles adhere to a simple structure consisting of an opening, a body, and a conclusion. A good opening introduces the topic, grabs the reader's attention, and leads into the body. The body should focus on the *five W's* plus *how*:

- What happened?
- When did it happen?
- Who was involved?
- Where did it happen?
- Why did it happen?
- How did it happen?

The conclusion of the article should be brief and contain a final point or idea for the reader.

While some articles in newspapers follow the same structure, straight news does not. In straight news, all or most of the *five W's* and *how* are usually covered in the lead, which is the opening of the article. The rest of the article supplies additional details from most important to least important. A conclusion is generally not used.

Activity 1 – Worksheet 25, "Get the Scoop!"

OBJECTIVE: Students are to select an event, observe it, and write a newspaper article about it.

PROCEDURE: A few days before this activity, ask your students to bring in copies of newspapers. After distributing and reviewing the words of List 25 and its sublist, hand out the newspapers. Allow students to work in small groups while examining the papers. Ask for volunteers to identify some of the parts, which might include sections on world news, local news, sports, finance and business, fashion, movie and TV listings, the obituaries, and the classifieds.

Hand out copies of Worksheet 25. Explain to your students that they are to select an event—perhaps a school sporting event, a dance, the ride home on the bus, lunch at the school cafeteria, an assembly, pretend they are reporters, observe the event, and write an article about it. Discuss the *five Ws* and *how* and encourage students to use the worksheet to help them organize their articles. Also encourage them to interview participants in the event. Background Sheet 25 can help students conduct effective interviews. Upon completion of the activity, you might wish to publish the articles in a class newspaper.

Activity 2 – Writing an Editorial

OBJECTIVE: Students are to select a meaningful topic and write an editorial.

PROCEDURE: Explain the difference between an editorial and a news article. Essentially, while a news article is written to impart facts or information, the purpose of an editorial is to persuade the reader to accept the author's viewpoints on an issue or topic.

Ask your students to volunteer some issues that concern them. Examples might include: strict parents; being misunderstood; too much homework; censorship; or local, national, or international controversies or events. List their ideas on the board or an overhead projector. Instruct your students to select an issue and write an editorial in which they try to convince their readers to accept their position. Encourage them to structure their editorials with an opening in which they introduce their issue, a body in which the issue is explained, and a closing in which they make a recommendation or call on the reader to take action. Upon completion of the activity, you might wish to publish some of the articles in a class or school newspaper.

Words of Newspapers and Magazines

People read newspapers, magazines, and on-line publications for information and entertainment. Because their readerships are usually diverse, most publications offer a variety of material. Even when a publication is aimed at a particular audience or subject, it may still carry many kinds of articles, features, and columns. Following are words associated with newspapers and magazines.

accuracy	feature	publisher
advertising	filler	query
anecdotes	foreign correspondent	readership
angle	free speech	reporter
AP (Associated Press)	freelance	Reuters
audience	headline	scoop
balance	human interest	sidebar
breaking story	information	slant
bureau	interview	source
byline	investigative reporter	staff
cartoons	lead story	straight news
circulation	libel	stringer
city desk	managing editor	style
column	news story	subject
copy editor	nonfiction	supplement
cover story	obituary	syndicated feature
dateline	on-line magazine	tabloid
deadline	op-ed	tip
edition	opinion	UPI (United Press International)
editor	photo essay	wire service
editorial	photographs	wire story
editor-in-chief	plagiarism	witness
entertainment	press conference	
facts	press release	

Sublist 25: Types of Articles and Columns Found in Newspapers and Magazines

book reviews	gardening	local news
business	general interest	movie reviews
classifieds	health	obituary
comics	historical	opinion
crafts	home repair	pets
editorials	how-to	politics
essays	human interest	profile
exposé	humor	psychology
fashion	informational	real estate
features	inspirational	science
fitness	interview	sports
food	investigative	theater reviews

Get the Scoop!

DIRECTIONS: Select a newsworthy event at school—perhaps a dance, football game, assembly, or special discussion. Imagine that you are a reporter. Attend the event, take notes, interview participants if possible, and write an article about the event. Build your article around the *five W's* and *how* by answering the following questions.

1. What was the event? _____

   _____

   _____

2. When did the event take place? _____

   _____

   _____

3. Where did it happen? _____

   _____

   _____

4. Who was involved? _____

   _____

   _____

5. Why did the event happen? _____

   _____

   _____

6. How did it happen? _____

   _____

   _____

7. What was the result of the event? _____

   _____

   _____

Background Sheet 25:
Tips for Effective Interviews

- For your interview, select someone who knows about your topic.

- Before the interview, gather background information on your topic and develop a list of questions to ask.

- Avoid using questions that can be answered by a simple yes or no; instead, ask questions that require explanations. Follow up interesting (or confusing) answers with additional questions.

- During the interview, listen carefully and write down important notes. Avoid trying to write down everything the person says. You won't be able to, and you will end up missing essential facts.

- If you are unsure of something, ask for clarification.

- If you want to quote someone, be sure to use the person's exact words.

- At the end of the interview, review important information with the interviewee.

- Always thank the person you interviewed for his or her time.

Science Words

TEACHING SUGGESTIONS

While not every student may aspire to be a scientist someday, all require fundamental knowledge of the subject if they hope to achieve a basic understanding of the workings of our world. List 26 provides words that the average student, especially the student who writes about science, should know.

Activity 1 – Worksheet 26, "Writing About Science"

OBJECTIVE: Students are to select a topic in science and write an essay explaining the topic and why it should (or should not) be taught in school.

PROCEDURE: Distribute copies of List 26 and review the words with your students. Emphasize how extensive the subject of science is, starting with the subatomic world and extending throughout the universe. Note that the words on the list represent only a small part of science.

Hand out copies of Worksheet 26. Explain that, for this activity, students are to select a topic in science and write an essay in which they explain the importance of the topic. They should also explain why the topic should be taught in school. Note that answering the questions on the worksheet will help your students to organize their ideas.

Activity 2 – Recording an Observation

OBJECTIVE: Students are to observe and record an event or experiment in science.

PROCEDURE: Distribute copies of List 26 and review the words with your students. For this activity your students are to observe an event, phenomenon, or experiment in science and write an account of it. For example, they might observe the changing colors of the sky as the sun sets, track an approaching storm (via the Internet), or watch a squirrel as it gathers nuts. They might instead simply record a science experiment that they performed in their science lab. Instruct your students to observe carefully and write accurately. They should include specific details.

See List 16, "Ecology Words," List 18, "Food Words," List 20, "Health Words," and List 23, "Math Words."

Science Words

It is impossible to understand existence without a basic understanding of science. The words of the following list are the starting point in attempting to comprehend our world.

absolute zero	biotechnology	concave
absorb	blood vessel	condensation
acceleration	boiling point	condense
acid rain	buoyancy	conduction
adaptation	calorie	coniferous
air pressure	carbohydrate	conservation
algae	carbon dioxide	constant
allergy	carcinogen	constellation
alloy	cardiovascular	consumer
amino acid	carnivore	continent
amoeba	catalyst	control
ampere	cell	conversion
amphibian	cellulose	convex
anatomy	Celsius scale	corrosion
animal	chemical reaction	cross-pollination
antibiotic	chemistry	cytoplasm
asexual	chlorophyll	decay
astronaut	chloroplast	deceleration
astronomer	cholesterol	decompose
astronomy	chromosome	decomposition
atmosphere	circuit	degree
atom	circulation	density
atomic number	classification	dependence
aurora	climate	depletion
bacteria	clone	dew
balance	cold-blooded	diatom
barometer	combustion	diffraction
behavior	comet	diffusion
benign	community	digestion
biologist	competition	disease
biology	compound	dissolve
biome	computer	distillation

DNA
dominant
Doppler effect
Earth
eclipse
ecology
ecosystem
egg
electricity
electrolyte
electromagnetic
electron
element
embryo
endangered species
energy
environment
enzyme
erosion
evaporation
evolution
exhale
exothermic
expand
extinct
Fahrenheit scale
fertile
fertilization
fetus
fiber optics
filament
fog
food chain
formula
fossil fuel
fracture

freezing point
frequency
friction
frost
fungus
galaxy
gas
gene
generator
genetic engineering
genome
geothermal energy
germination
glacier
glucose
gravity
habitat
half-life
hatch
heat
herbivore
heterogeneous
hibernation
homeostasis
homogeneous
hormone
host
human being
hurricane
hybrid
hydrocarbon
hydroelectric
hypothesis
igneous
immunity
incandescent

incubate
induction
inert
inertia
infection
infrared
inhale
inorganic
insect
insoluble
instinct
invertebrate
ion
isotope
jet stream
Kelvin scale
kingdom
larva
lava
liquid
machine
magma
magnet
magnetism
mammal
mantle
marine life
marsupial
mass
matter
melting point
membrane
metabolism
metamorphosis
meteor
microbiology

Science Words *(continued)*

microorganism	property	spectrum
microscope	protein	sperm
migration	proton	star
molecule	protoplasm	static electricity
moon	protozoan	subatomic particle
mutation	quark	suspension
nuclear energy	radiation	symbiosis
nucleus	radioactivity	system
omnivore	reactor	table
orbit	recessive	temperature
organic	recycle	theory
organism	reflection	thermometer
osmosis	refraction	thrust
oxygen	regeneration	tide
ozone	reproduction	trait
parasite	respiration	transistor
particle accelerator	revolve	transmutation
periodic table	RNA	tumor
peristalsis	satellite	ultrasonic
permafrost	scale	ultraviolet ray
photon	scavenger	universe
photosynthesis	scientific method	vaccine
phylum	season	vaporization
physics	sedimentary	variable
planet	seismic	variation
plankton	self-pollination	velocity
plant	semiconductor	vertebrate
polarity	smog	virus
pollen	solar energy	viscosity
pollination	solar system	voltage
pollution	solid	warm-blooded
population	solution	water vapor
precipitation	solvent	watt
predator	sound	wave
prey	space	wavelength
primate	species	weight

Writing About Science

DIRECTIONS: Select a topic in science. Answer the questions that follow and write an essay explaining why this topic should or should not be taught in school.

1. What is your topic? _____

   _____

2. Describe this topic. _____

   _____

   _____

   _____

   _____

   _____

   _____

3. How is this topic important? _____

   _____

   _____

   _____

   _____

   _____

   _____

4. Why should (or should not) this topic be taught in school? _____

   _____

   _____

   _____

   _____

   _____

   _____

   _____

27

Sports Words

TEACHING SUGGESTIONS

Most people participate in sports for the challenge of competition, for enjoyment, or for relaxation. It is likely that many of your students enjoy one or more sports. This enjoyment can be a springboard for writing ideas.

Activity 1 – Worksheet 27, "The Rules and Strategies of the Game"

OBJECTIVE: Students are to select a favorite sport and write a descriptive account of it.

PROCEDURE: Distribute copies of List 27 to your students and review the sports words. Ask for volunteers to briefly describe the sports they enjoy.

For this activity, hand out copies of Worksheet 27. Instruct your students to select one of their favorite sports and write a description of how they participate in it. They should include an explanation of its rules and strategies. Answering the questions on the worksheet will help students focus their ideas before writing.

Activity 2 – Being a Sportswriter

OBJECTIVE: Students are to attend a school sporting event and write an article about it.

PROCEDURE: A few days in advance of this activity, you might wish to ask students to bring in the sports sections of various newspapers. Allow some time in class for them to examine the articles. Point out some of the features of the articles—they have headlines, are usually written in short sentences, may include interviews or quotes from some of the people involved, and will contain the scores and other facts about the contest.

Instruct your students to attend a school sporting event of their choice and write an article about it. Encourage them to take notes during the event so that they will have all the important facts and details.

See List 25, "Words of Newspapers and Magazines."

Sports Words

The thrill of competition stirs most people. Sports offer the opportunity to test our athletic powers as well as have fun. Following are words that are related to sports.

archery
athlete
auto racing
badminton
ballooning
baseball
basketball
bicycling
billiards
boat racing
body building
bowling
boxing
bullfighting
canoeing
championship
coach
commentators
competition
conditioning
equipment
exercise
fans
fencing
field hockey
fishing
fitness
football
game
gold
gymnastics
handball

hang gliding
harness racing
horseback riding
horseshoes
hunting
ice hockey
ice sailing
ice skating
judge
judo
karate
kayaking
lacrosse
loser
marathon
match
motorcycle racing
mountain climbing
official
opponent
playoff
practice
racquetball
rafting
referee
rowing
rugby
rules
running
sailing
scuba diving
skiing

sky diving
snowmobiling
soccer
softball
spectators
speed boating
squash
superstar
surfing
swimming
team
teammate
tennis
track and field
training
trophy
umpire
volleyball
water skiing
weight lifting
winner
wrestling
yachting

The Rules and Strategies of the Game

DIRECTIONS: Think of a sport that you enjoy either as a participant or a spectator. Answer the questions below and then write a description of the rules of your sport and how the game is played.

1. What sport did you choose? _____

_____

2. Why do you enjoy this sport? _____

_____

_____

_____

_____

3. Are you a participant, spectator, or both? Explain. _____

_____

_____

_____

_____

4. What are the rules of this sport? _____

_____

_____

_____

_____

_____

5. What are the basic strategies? _____

_____

_____

_____

_____

_____

Travel Words

TEACHING SUGGESTIONS

We are a mobile people. We like to travel. With modern transportation we can travel long distances quickly and at a reasonable cost. Whether on a business trip, vacation, or simply sightseeing on a Sunday afternoon, wherever one goes, traveling offers new experiences. These experiences can be the inspiration for students' writings.

Activity 1 – Worksheet 28, "Traveling Around"

OBJECTIVE: Students are to write an account of a trip they recently took.

PROCEDURE: Hand out copies of List 28 and review the travel words with your students. Many will be familiar, but you should explain any that are new to anyone.

Next, distribute copies of Worksheet 28. Instruct your students to think of a trip they took recently. It might have been a vacation or merely a day trip to visit a relative or friend. They are to complete the worksheet, which will help them to clarify and organize their thoughts, and then write an account about their trip.

Activity 2 – Taking an Imaginary Trip

OBJECTIVE: Students are to write an account of an imaginary trip.

PROCEDURE: Ask your students to think of a place they would like to visit. It can be anywhere— a distant city or even the moon. Why do they want to go there? Who would they take if they could invite someone to go with them? What things would they take? What would they expect to see? How would they get there and how would they return? They are to write a descriptive account of their imaginary trip.

Travel Words

With modern transportation, people are traveling to distant places more than ever. The following words are the stock of the travel writer.

abroad	entertainment	relaxation
accommodations	fare	rent
adventure	first class	reservation
airline	gratuity	resort
airplane	guide	round trip
airport	hotel	ship
backpack	immunization	sightseeing
bed and breakfast	inn	ticket
bellhop	itinerary	time sharing
booking	luggage	time zone
bumping	meal plan	tour
bus	motel	tourist
cancellation	motor lodge	train
car	off-season	transfer
charter	overseas	travel agent
credit card	package tour	travel brochure
cruise	passport	traveler's check
currency	plans	trip
customs	rates	vacation
destination	recreation	visa

Traveling Around

DIRECTIONS: Think of a trip you recently took. It might have been a trip with your parents or friends, a class trip, or one you took alone. Complete this worksheet and write an account of your trip.

1. Where did you go? _____

   _____

2. When did you go? _____

   _____

3. Why did you go? _____

   _____

   _____

4. Who went with you? _____

   _____

   _____

5. What did you take along? _____

   _____

   _____

   _____

6. Describe some of the things you saw or visited. _____

   _____

   _____

   _____

7. What was the most memorable event of your trip? _____

   _____

   _____

   _____

LISTS AND ACTIVITIES FOR
Fiction Writing

29

Words of Adventure and Romance

TEACHING SUGGESTIONS

Most people like stories of adventure and romance. Because of their popularity with students, adventures and romances provide a fertile field for writing activities.

Activity 1 – Worksheet 29, "The Continuing Adventures of . . ."

OBJECTIVE: Students are to select a favorite character from an adventure or romance story and write a new story for that character.

PROCEDURE: Distribute copies of List 29 and review the words with your students. Explain that all of these words may be found in stories of adventure or romance. Ask your students to name some examples of these kinds of stories. Encourage them to name books as well as movies. Note that many stories are a combination of adventure and romance and that most rely on fast action and interesting characters. The best stories are exciting and absorbing, and the reader or viewer usually winds up rooting for the good guys.

To begin the activity, hand out copies of Worksheet 29. Instruct your students to complete the worksheet first, then write their stories.

EXTENSION: Ask your students to create a new hero or heroine and to write an adventure or romance story.

Activity 2 – Writing About the Complete Character

OBJECTIVE: Students are to select a character from a favorite adventure or romance story and write a descriptive account of that character.

PROCEDURE: Hand out copies of List 29 and review the words with your students. Explain that the lead characters of adventures and romances are usually handsome or beautiful and possess considerable personal magnetism. They are designed to capture the interest of the reader or viewer. Moreover, they often find themselves in exotic settings and seemingly hopeless situations. The story's appeal is centered around the characters as readers or viewers want to find out what happens next to the characters.

For this assignment, students are to choose a favorite character from an adventure or romance and write a descriptive account of that character. Encourage your students to briefly summarize the story from which they took the character, describe the character physically and emotionally, and then tell what they feel is the character's most appealing trait.

See List 33, "Words of Science Fiction and Fantasy," List 35, "Spy, Detective, and Mystery Words," and List 36, "Western Words."

Words of Adventure and Romance

Cliffhangers, chase scenes, impossible escapes, excitement, and love are the ingredients of adventure and romance stories. These tales usually have clear-cut heroes, heroines, and villains, making it easy to root for the good guys. Adventure and romance make up a large part of the published fiction every year, and the stories can be as much fun to write as they are to read. The following list contains words you will find in stories of adventure and romance.

abduct	emotion	kiss
agent	evil	leave
anxiety	feeling	let down
apprehension	find	lie
arouse	flirt	lips
beautiful	foolish	lose
beloved	forbidden	love
betray	forgiven	lovely
bold	girlfriend	lover
boyfriend	goodbye	lover's triangle
breakup	good-looking	lovesick
broken heart	grief	lusty
brutality	grin	marry
chase	handsome	melancholy
confidence	happy	miss
confusion	heartbreak	mourn
crafty	heartless	need
cruel	hero	nervous
cry	heroine	obstacle
danger	hostage	passion
defensive	hug	peril
depression	humorous	pine
desire	ignore	plan
despair	interest	possess
divorce	jilt	pout
double-cross	joy	protect
ecstasy	kidnap	ransom
embrace	kill	rapture

Words of Adventure and Romance *(continued)*

reconcile	smile	trap
regret	sneaky	trick
remorse	snuggle	true
rescue	soft	trust
resent	startle	tryst
revenge	steal	two-timer
ruin	stubborn	villain
save	suicide	uncertain
scheme	sympathy	want
scorn	tears	warm
search	tease	warn
security	tender	waver
seductive	thwart	wicked
seek	timid	wish
shrewd	torture	willful
sigh	tragic	

The Continuing Adventures of . . .

DIRECTIONS: Think of a favorite character from an adventure or romance story. You may have read the story in a book or seen it in the movies or on TV. After completing this worksheet, write a new story for your character.

1. Who is your character? _____

2. Why did you choose this character? _____

_____

_____

_____

3. Describe your character's personality. _____

_____

_____

_____

_____

_____

4. Describe your character's physical traits. _____

_____

_____

_____

_____

_____

5. Briefly summarize your story. _____

_____

_____

_____

_____

_____

30

Words of Folklore

TEACHING SUGGESTIONS

The word *folklore* is like an umbrella. It covers several types of narrative prose found throughout the oral traditions of the world. While folklore includes myths, legends, fairy tales, tall tales, fables, and songs, the following list is limited to American folktales. Generally, folklore is highly creative and often interweaves truth and imagination. Folklore may pass in and out of written literature and may contain morals or lessons. The stories invariably offer a unique insight into the people who invented them. When teaching folklore, try reading some stories out loud to your students. Modeling can be an effective teaching technique and help your activity get off to a strong start.

Activity 1 – Worksheet 30, "Inventing a Folktale"

OBJECTIVE: Students are to write a modern folktale.

PROCEDURE: Distribute copies of List 30 and review the words with your students. Briefly discuss the scope of folklore and go over the included sublist. It is likely that most students will be familiar with many of the characters on the list. (You might wish to obtain an anthology of folktales from your library and keep it in the classroom for reference during your study of folklore.) Explain that many of the American folk stories focused on characters who had specific occupations. Paul Bunyan was a lumberjack, John Henry was a railroad man, and Annie Oakley was a sharpshooter.

To begin this assignment, hand out copies of Worksheet 30. Instruct your students to select a modern occupation and write a modern folktale about it, using the worksheet to organize their ideas. At the end of the activity, you may consider compiling a class *Folktale Book*.

Activity 2 – A Local Legend

OBJECTIVE: Students are to invent a local legend.

PROCEDURE: Most towns have individuals, events, or points of interest that strangers would find fascinating. Ask your students to think of a special person, place, or event in their town or in another town and write about him, her, or it. In their writing, they should describe their subject, its importance, and background.

See List 31, "Words of Mythology."

Words of Folklore

Folklore, which includes myths, legends, fairy tales, fables, tall tales, and songs, tells of the lives, traditions, and customs of people. Folklore mixes fantasy with fact and symbolism with reality, and it offers a special glimpse of the people who first told "them" tales.

backwoodsman	fearless	mighty	steadfast
ballad	feud	miner	steamboat
bandit	fiddler	miracle	steelworker
belief	fight	moonshine	storm
boast	fisherman	mountain man	strength
brag	folly	myth	strong
brave	frontier	outlaw	sturdy
calamity	frontiersman	pioneer	superstition
captain	fury	preacher	sweetheart
courageous	hardy	prospector	teamster
cowboy	heritage	railroad man	timber
cowgirl	honor	river pilot	tough
culture	hunter	rustler	tradition
custom	independent	saga	trapper
daring	Indian	sailor	traveler
duel	laborer	sayings	twister
exaggeration	lawman	scout	wagon train
exploits	legend	sharpshooter	wander
explorer	liar	sheepherder	Wild West
faithful	lonesome	soldier	wilderness
fanciful	loyal	spirit	wisdom
farmer	lumberjack	squaw	Yankee

Sublist 30: Who's Who in American Folklore

Johnny Appleseed – early conservationist

Sam Bass – good outlaw

Judge Roy Bean – frontier judge

Billy the Kid – young outlaw

Buffalo Bill – frontiersman

Daniel Boone – frontiersman

Jim Bridger – frontier scout

Strap Buckner – brawler

Paul Bunyan – lumberjack

Calamity Jane – frontierswoman

Kit Carson – frontier scout

Davy Crockett – frontiersman

Wyatt Earp – marshal

Febold Feboldson – pioneer

Mike Fink – frontier scout

John Henry – railroad man

Wild Bill Hickok – frontiersman

Doc Holliday – gunslinging doctor

Mose Humphreys – fireman

Johnny Inkslinger – bookkeeper

Jesse James – outlaw

Casey Jones – railroad engineer

Joe Magarac – steelman

Annie Oakley – sharpshooter

Old Stormalong – sailor

Pecos Bill – cowboy

Pocahontas – Indian woman

Paul Revere – colonial messenger

Sacajawea – Indian guide

John Smith – adventurer

Miles Standish and Priscilla – New World couple

Rip Van Winkle – sleepyhead

Inventing a Folktale

DIRECTIONS: American folklore often focuses on the occupations and lifestyles of an emerging nation. Think of an occupation of today, invent an imaginary character, and write a modern folktale about this character. Remember that folktales interweave elements of reality and imagination, and are usually sprinkled with exaggeration. Answering the questions below will help you to organize your thoughts.

1. What occupation did you choose? _____

2. What is your character's name? _____

   _____

3. Describe your character. _____

   _____

   _____

   _____

   _____

   _____

4. Describe your character's occupation. _____

   _____

   _____

   _____

   _____

   _____

5. In what ways does this occupation benefit people? _____

   _____

   _____

   _____

   _____

   _____

31

Words of Mythology

TEACHING SUGGESTIONS

Before science, the world was explained through mythology. Most ancient people invented elaborate myths in their attempts to explain where they came from and why the world behaved as it did. Although now we explain much of our world with science, myths still make for interesting reading and can provide fine topics for writing.

Activity 1 – Worksheet 31, "A Modern Myth"

OBJECTIVE: Students are to select a topic and write a modern myth.

PROCEDURE: Distribute copies of List 31 and review the words with your students. Briefly discuss the characteristics of myths and emphasize that ancient people invented myths to explain things in nature or behavior that they couldn't explain any other way.

Next, hand out copies of Worksheet 31. Ask your students to think of a modern problem associated with young people. You might suggest some of the following:

- Why students don't like homework.
- Why younger brothers or sisters like to annoy their older siblings.
- Why parents misunderstand their teenaged children.

Ask your students to suggest more potential topics, which you might list on the board or an overhead projector. Instruct students to select one of these topics, complete the worksheet to organize their thoughts, and write a modern myth about their topic. At the end of the activity, you might want to compile a class book of modern mythology.

Activity 2 – Writing Nature Myths

OBJECTIVE: Students are to select a phenomenon in nature and write a myth.

PROCEDURE: Ask your students to name some phenomena of nature. Some possibilities include rain, violent storms, day and night, snow, and why stars twinkle. Instruct them to choose a topic from nature and write a myth explaining why nature behaves in this way.

See List 30, "Words of Folklore."

Words of Mythology

To explain their world, ancient people invented myths. They told stories of how the world was created, how humans and animals came into being, how natural phenomena occurred, and how and why human customs and practices developed. Many myths refer to gods, goddesses, supernatural creatures, and cataclysmic events. Following are some words associated with myths.

afterlife	fairy	magic	serpent
Amazons	fate	Medusa	shaman
amulet	feat	mermaid	siren
battle	fertility	Minotaur	sorcerer
brownies	genie	mysticism	sorceress
centaurs	ghost	Narcissus	spell
chaos	giant	nemesis	spirit
charm	goddess	night	sprite
contest	god	nymph	supernatural
creation	gremlin	odyssey	taboo
cult	griffin	ogre	test
Cyclops	Hades	omen	thunderbolt
demigod	heaven	oracle	Titan
destiny	hero	Phoenix	trick
destruction	heroine	prince	troll
divine	idol	princess	underworld
dragon	immortal	queen	unicorn
dwarf	incantation	quest	warlord
elf	king	riddle	winged horse
epic	leprechaun	sacrifice	witch
evil spirit	lightning	sea monster	wizard

A Modern Myth

DIRECTIONS: Ancient people invented myths in an attempt to explain the unexplainable. Select a topic or problem such as:

- Why students don't like homework.
- Why younger brothers or sisters like to annoy their older siblings.
- Why parents misunderstand their teenaged children.

Complete this worksheet, then write a modern myth.

1. Describe the topic of your myth. _____

   _____

   _____

   _____

2. Describe the characters you will use in your myth. _____

   _____

   _____

   _____

   _____

   _____

   _____

   _____

3. Describe how your myth will explain your topic. _____

   _____

   _____

   _____

   _____

   _____

THE WRITING TEACHER'S BOOK OF LISTS

Words of Plays

TEACHING SUGGESTIONS

Plays are a distinct form of literature. Since a play is performed on stage, the playwright must take into account the visual dramatic appeal of his or her work. Playwrights must carefully consider what they want to say and how to say it. While plays may evolve during the writing process, effective prewriting can make the overall task of writing the play easier.

Activity 1 – Worksheet 32, "Writing a Play"

OBJECTIVE: Students are to select a topic and write a play of at least one act.

PROCEDURE: Distribute copies of List 32 and review the words with your students. Explain that plays are a special type of literature and that they have a unique structure. Like any good story, a play revolves around characters, conflict, and action. In a play, the main character, or protagonist, is confronted with a problem. As the character tries to solve the problem, he or she encounters one or more obstacles that complicate his or her options, which results in conflict. The problem usually grows worse. At the end of the play, through the character's resources, he or she manages to overcome the problem, with the consequence being a happy ending. In some plays, the characters are unable to solve the problem, and, depending on the degree of the unhappy ending, the play may be considered a tragedy.

Before beginning this activity, hand out copies of Background Sheet 32a, which offers a simple formula for plotting a play, and Background Sheet 32b, which offers an example of a play format. Discuss the formula and example with your students. Emphasize that while a play is composed of parts, all of the parts must be organized into a whole. Everything must lead to the climax.

For the assignment, hand out copies of Worksheet 32. Instruct your students to select a topic—a first date, a school election, the pressures of being a student, or a special event. They are to complete the worksheet and write a play of at least one act based on their topic. Perhaps you can arrange for students to perform some of their plays.

EXTENSION: Instruct your students to complete the example of the play on Background Sheet 32b.

Activity 2 – Reviewing a Play

OBJECTIVE: Students are to watch and write a review of a play.

PROCEDURE: For this activity your students will need to attend a play, or watch a play on TV. (Perhaps a class trip can be arranged to attend a play, or students may be able to watch a play on public television. Some PBS stations broadcast plays from time to time.) Begin the activity by distributing copies of List 32, Background Sheet 32a, and Background Sheet 32b. Discuss the words, structure, and format of plays.

For the activity, instruct your students to watch a play and write a review of it, discussing its structure, plot, and overall quality.

See List 34, "Words of Screenplays."

Words of Plays

Plays are a powerful medium of communication. They enable the playwright to dramatically show his or her interpretation of life to the audience. Following are words associated with plays.

acoustics	dialogue	protagonist
act	director	rehearsal
action	drama	resolution
actor	event	role
actress	irony	romance
audience	lead	scene
cast	melodrama	segment
characters	monologue	set
climax	musical	soliloquy
comedy	narrator	stage
complications	obstacle	star
conflict	opening	suspense
costumes	playwright	symbolism
crisis	plot	theatre
curtain	producer	tragedy
designs	production	villain

Writing a Play

DIRECTIONS: Choose a topic, for example, a first date, a school election, the pressures of being a student, or a special event. Answer the questions below; then write a play of at least one act about your topic.

1. What is the topic of your play? _____

   _____

   _____

2. Who are the lead characters? _____

   _____

   _____

3. Describe the problem the characters face. _____

   _____

   _____

4. What obstacle(s) prevents the characters from solving the problem? _____

   _____

   _____

   _____

5. What complications arise in the play? _____

   _____

   _____

   _____

6. Describe the climax. _____

   _____

   _____

7. Describe the resolution. _____

   _____

   _____

   _____

Background Sheet 32a:
A Simple Structure for a Play

The following guidelines provide the basic structure for writing a play.

1. *Opening:* Background is offered and a description of the situation is given. A problem (or a potential problem) is revealed.

2. *Plan:* The main character devises a plan to solve the problem and achieve a goal.

3. *Obstacle:* Obstacles arise that add to the problem; this causes conflict.

4. *Complications:* The problem grows and the character continues seeking a solution. The character devises more plans.

5. *Climax:* The character finally solves the problem, or he or she realizes that the problem cannot be solved.

6. *Resolution:* As a result of solving the problem, the character achieves his or her goal; or because the problem could not be solved, the character realizes that the goal is unattainable.

A play can be expanded to several acts and scenes, but the basic structure remains the same.

Background Sheet 32b:
Play Format

Plays are a special form of literature, which have a special format. Here are some general rules for format,* followed by the beginning of a sample play in which a girl is trying to figure out a way to meet a new boy in school. Her friend offers a suggestion.

1. A play begins with a title.

2. A list of characters is necessary.

3. ACTS and scenes must be labeled.

4. The SETTING is described. Depending on the play, this may be brief or detailed.

5. AT RISE refers to the action that is happening on stage as the curtain rises.

6. CHARACTER names are typed in capital letters and followed by colons. Stage directions are written in parentheses to make them distinct from the character's words. Dialogue is generally single-spaced, with double-spacing between speakers.

7. Longer stage directions or descriptions are usually separated from the dialogue and are single-spaced.

8. The word CURTAIN is used to indicate the ending of a scene.

*The format here is commonly used in schools. Professional playwrights use a slightly different format, which can be found in books on play writing.

THE WRITING TEACHER'S BOOK OF LISTS

Following is the beginning of a sample play entitled *The First Date*.

Characters

Meg, a fifteen-year-old girl
Jill, her friend
(Note: More characters would be added.)

ACT I
Scene 1

SETTING: Girls' locker room.

AT RISE: Meg and Jill have just finished cheerleading practice. Meg sits on a bench; she looks forlorn. Jill is putting a pompon in her locker.

MEG (dreamily):   I wish I could get to know him.

JILL: Who?

MEG: Eric. . . . Eric Peters. The new junior. I don't think he knows I'm alive.

JILL: Sure he does. He was staring at you in physics today. (She closes her locker and turns to Meg; looks at her thoughtfully.)

MEG (frowning):   He was looking at the chalkboard. I was in the way.

JILL: You'll never get to know him if you keep being so negative.

MEG: It's hard not to be negative when you don't have a chance.

JILL (sympathetically):   Well, then we just have to make things more positive. Next week's my birthday party.

MEG (curiously):   Yeah?

JILL: You're coming, right?

MEG: You know that.

JILL: Good, so I'll invite Eric, and I'll make sure that I get you together.

MEG: But you don't know him any better than I do.

JILL: That's where being positive comes in. He won't come unless I invite him. (She smiles confidently.) Let's go.

Words of Science Fiction and Fantasy

TEACHING SUGGESTIONS

Science fiction and fantasy constitute major genres of literature. They are broad categories in which the lines of distinction are often blurred. Indeed, some authors prefer to call the entire realm "speculative fiction." For the purposes of this book, two sublists are provided, one for science fiction and the other for fantasy. While the differences between the two can sometimes blend together, science fiction most often focuses on stories that take place in the future and have a distinct technological setting or theme. Fantasy is more apt to center on magic and the supernatural.

Activity 1 – Worksheet 33, "A Story About the Fantastic"

OBJECTIVE: Students are to write a science fiction or fantasy story.

PROCEDURE: Distribute copies of List 33 and review the words with your students. Note that good examples of science fiction are any of the "Star Wars" or "Star Trek" stories, while equally solid examples of fantasy include J.R.R. Tolkien's *The Lord of the Rings* trilogy, Ray Bradbury's *Something Wicked This Way Comes,* and C.S. Lewis's *The Chronicles of Narnia.* Discuss the differences between science fiction and fantasy, but point out that some stories do not fit neatly into either category. Also point out that, while these stories are about future or magical events and strange places, plotting and characterization must be consistent and believable.

Hand out copies of Worksheet 33. Note that completing the worksheet will help students develop their stories.

Activity 2 – Reviewing Science Fiction or Fantasy

OBJECTIVE: Students are to write a review of a favorite science fiction or fantasy story or movie.

PROCEDURE: Distribute copies of List 33 and briefly review the words with your students. Ask for volunteers to name some memorable science fiction or fantasy stories or movies. Ask students what they liked about these stories and highlight the differences between the genres.

For the assignment, students are to choose a favorite story or movie of science fiction or fantasy and write a review. Encourage them to include a summary of the plot, a description of the characters, and what they felt were the best parts of the story, as well as any weaknesses. Remind them to support their ideas with details.

See List 29, "Words of Adventure and Romance," List 35, "Spy, Detective, and Mystery Words," and List 36, "Western Words."

Words of Science Fiction and Fantasy

Distant worlds and times, magic, and the supernatural compose the realm of speculative fiction. While science fiction and fantasy are often grouped together under this broad term, for clarity and convenience they are presented in separate lists here.

The stories that fall into these categories can fire our imaginations with scenes and visions of the strange, the beautiful, and the wonderful. They can expand our horizons by showing us glimpses of what might have been, what might be, or what actually is, although we don't recognize it.

WORDS OF SCIENCE FICTION

abduction	future	orbit
alien	galactic empire	organism
android	galaxy	parallel world
Armageddon	hologram	planet
artificial environment	humanoid	planetfall
artificial intelligence	intergalactic	probe
asteroid	interplanetary	ray gun
astronaut	interstellar	reentry
automation	invention	robot
bionic	invisibility	rocket
black hole	journey	satellite
blast off	landing	scientist
clone	laser	sensor
computer	life form	solar system
cosmos	life-support system	space colony
creature	light year	space drive
cyborg	light-speed	space port
death ray	lost race	space station
device	lost world	space warp
dimension	lunar colony	spaceship
Earth	machine	spacesuit
enclosed cities	malfunction	star
eternity	mind swap	starship
exploration	mission	submarine
extraterrestrial	moon	sun
flying saucer	moon base	symbiosis
force field	mutant	takeoff

Words of Science Fiction and Fantasy *(continued)*

technology

telepathy

teleportation

terrestrial

time travel

time warp

UFO (Unidentified Flying Object)

universe

voyage

wormhole

WORDS OF FANTASY

amulet

apparition

armor

banshee

barbarian

beast

bewitch

binding

castle

changeling

chant

charm

conjure

crone

deed

demon

destiny

divination

dragon

dryad

elf

enchanter

enchantress

exorcism

fairy

familiar

fate

fortune

genie

ghost

giant

gnome

goblin

goddess

god

haunt

hero

incantation

king

lance

macabre

magic

magic carpet

magic lamp

magic wand

medium

monster

necromancy

nymph

occult

ogre

omen

pentagram

phantom

pixie

possess

potion

prince

princess

queen

rite

ritual

rune

sacrifice

séance

shape-shifting

shield

slay

sorcerer

sorceress

sorcery

soul

specter

spell

sprite

stake

sword

talisman

trance

troll

vampire

ward

warlock

warrior

witch

witchcraft

wizard

wonder worker

A Story About the Fantastic

DIRECTIONS: Complete the worksheet and write a science fiction or fantasy story.

1. Describe your main characters. _____

   _____

   _____

   _____

   _____

2. Describe the setting of your story. _____

   _____

   _____

   _____

   _____

3. Describe the main conflict. _____

   _____

   _____

   _____

   _____

4. Briefly summarize the plot. _____

   _____

   _____

   _____

   _____

5. Describe the climax. _____

   _____

   _____

   _____

   _____

Words of Screenplays

TEACHING SUGGESTIONS

Stories written for television or the movies are called *screenplays*. They are written in a special format, often referred to as a *script*. With the availability of video cameras, it is possible for students to write and produce simple screenplays.

Activity 1 – Worksheet 34, "My Movie"

OBJECTIVE: Students are to write and videotape a screenplay.

PROCEDURE: Distribute copies of List 34 and explain that a screenplay is a story written for television or the movies. Discuss the vocabulary. Also hand out copies of Background Sheet 34, which contains information for setting up a screenplay as well as a sample. Discuss the information with your students.

Next, distribute copies of Worksheet 34. Explain that for the assignment, students are to write a screenplay. Suggest that they select a familiar topic, for example, a school scene, which will not require an elaborate set or props. Note that they should limit their material for a screenplay to between three to five minutes.

After students have finished writing their screenplays, you may prefer to select four or five of the best (or all), and permit students to produce them. The writers of each screenplay should arrange for students to play the roles, obtain any necessary props, and, of course, rehearse their lines. Videotape the stories, and show them to the class.

EXTENSION: Instruct your students to complete the sample of the screenplay on Background Sheet 34.

Activity 2 – Being a Critic of the Big Screen

OBJECTIVE: Students are to watch and write a review of a movie or TV show.

PROCEDURE: Instruct your students to choose a movie or TV show, watch the broadcast, and write a review. In their reviews, they should consider the story line, characters, dialogue, action, sets, and costumes. Encourage them to offer their opinions on how the production might have been improved.
    See List 32, "Words of Plays."

Words of Screenplays

A screenplay is a story written for television or the movies. Following is a sampling of the special vocabulary screenwriters use.

angle on – the view on which the camera is focused

back to – a return to the previous scene

close-up – a close shot

cut to – to make the picture on one camera give way instantly to the picture on another camera

dissolve – to make the picture on one camera gradually disappear and replace it with another

ext. – abbreviation for *exterior,* a designation of where a scene takes place

fade in – to make a picture appear gradually

fade out – to make a picture disappear gradually

favoring – a shot focusing on one character in a group

insert – a shot of something inserted into the scene; for example, a letter

int. – abbreviation for *interior,* a designation of where a scene takes place

long shot – a camera shot of an entire scene

pan – a camera shot that follows action by moving from side to side

pov – a character's point of view; what the character sees

vo – voice over; a scene in which a character's voice is heard but he or she is not seen

My Movie

DIRECTIONS: Write a screenplay on a topic of your choice. Complete this worksheet first to organize your thoughts.

1. What is the topic of your screenplay? _____

   _____

2. Describe your setting. _____

   _____

   _____

   _____

   _____

3. Describe the lead characters. _____

   _____

   _____

   _____

   _____

   _____

4. Describe the plot of your screenplay. _____

   _____

   _____

   _____

   _____

   _____

5. Describe the climax of your screenplay. _____

   _____

   _____

   _____

Background Sheet 34:
Screenplay Format

Following is a format for writing screenplays. Also included as a sample is the beginning of a screenplay.

1. Begin with your title.

2. ACTS are capitalized and numbered.

3. Scenes are numbered.

4. CAMERA DIRECTIONS and names of CHARACTERS are capitalized.

5. Character names are centered for dialogue.

6. Dialogue is indented and appears below the character's name. Brief character descriptions appear in parentheses centered below the character's name. Dialogue is single-spaced.

7. Scene descriptions begin at the margin and are single-spaced.

8. Double-spacing is used between scenes, between the words of different characters, and between dialogue and scene descriptions.

9. Acts usually begin with FADE IN and end with FADE OUT.

10. At the conclusion of the screenplay, use THE END.

Following is the beginning of a sample screenplay.

House of Demons

ACT I

FADE IN:
1 EXT., NIGHT, YARD OF OLD, RUN-DOWN VICTORIAN HOUSE

House is deteriorated with broken windows, sagging porch. In dim moonlight it appears to have been abandoned for many years. The scene is spooky, haunting. The yard is overgrown with weeds, twisted trees, and thorn bushes. Three teenagers, JIMMY SANTOS, BRIAN MATHEWS, AND LIZ EDWARDS are standing at the edge of the yard, looking at the house.

2 ANGLE ON TEENS

LIZ
(nervously)

Let's go. This isn't a good idea.

BRIAN
(calmly)

No, according to the legend, treasure's in there.

JIMMY
(uncertainly)

Yeah . . . and so are demons. What about those treasure hunters last year? They were lucky to get out of there alive.

BRIAN

You don't really believe that stuff. Old man Carter only told those stories to keep people away while he was alive. He was a hermit . . . crazy as a loon.

LIZ

But what about the treasure?

Background Sheet 34 *(continued)*

BRIAN

Carter inherited it from his father. He never spent a dime.

LIZ
(shaking her head)

The place gives me the creeps.

BRIAN

Look, your dad lost his job. And because of that your folks are going to lose their house. This is a way you can help them.

JIMMY

How are you so sure about the treasure?

3 FAVORING BRIAN

BRIAN takes a piece of paper out of his jacket pocket. He opens it.

4 INSERT PAPER

The moonlight shows it to be a map.

5 SHOT OF TEENS, FAVORING BRIAN

BRIAN
(smiling)

This tells us right where the treasure is . . .

35

Spy, Detective, and Mystery Words

TEACHING SUGGESTIONS

One of the reasons spy, detective, and mystery stories have maintained their popularity over the years is the element of reader involvement. Trying to guess who is responsible for the crime or rooting for the hero to outsmart the enemy agents—along with solid action—keeps the reader interested and makes him or her want to find out what happens next. List 35 provides words you will find in stories of this genre.

Activity 1 – Worksheet 35, "Creating a Hero"

OBJECTIVE: Students are to create a fictional spy or detective hero.

PROCEDURE: Distribute copies of List 35 and review the words with your students. It is likely that they will be familiar with most of the words. Explain any that are unfamiliar. Ask your students to name some famous spies or detectives in real life, in literature, on TV, or in the movies. It is probable that James Bond, Sherlock Holmes, Miss Marple, J.B. Fletcher, the Hardy Boys, Nancy Drew, or perhaps even Encyclopedia Brown will be suggested.

For the assignment, tell your students that they will be creating their own spy or detective characters. Hand out copies of Worksheet 35, noting that completing the worksheet will help students develop their characters.

EXTENSION: You may suggest that your students write a story in which their newly created character plays a lead role.

Activity 2 – A Mysterious Occurrence

OBJECTIVE: Students are to write an account of a mysterious occurrence.

PROCEDURE: Distribute copies of List 35 and review the words with your students. To start this activity, ask your students if they have ever been involved in or heard about a mysterious event. Most people have experienced inexplicable events at one time or another.

Instruct your students to write about this event. They should include what happened, when and where the event occurred, why it happened (if they know), who was involved, and what happened afterward. Perhaps the event remains a mystery.

See List 29, "Words of Adventure and Romance," List 33, "Words of Science Fiction and Fantasy," and List 36, "Western Words."

Spy, Detective, and Mystery Words

Few stories involve the reader as much as a good spy tale, detective yarn, or mystery. These stories usually allow the reader to become a partner with the hero as he or she tries to solve the crime or outwit the bad guys. Here are some words writers use for this genre.

accomplice	counterintelligence	infiltrate	risk
analyze	court	innocent	robbery
anguish	covert	intuition	ruthless
assassination	crime	investigate	secret
attorney	criminal	jail	security
blackmail	deduction	judge	sentence
bloodstain	DNA evidence	jury	set free
blowup	double agent	justice	smuggle
bomb	escape	kill	society
boss	evidence	law	solution
break-in	execution	lawyer	stakeout
bribe	explosion	legal	steal
brutality	fact	lie	suicide
bug	FBI (Federal	loan shark	surveillance
burglar	Bureau of	mob	suspect
bust	Investigation)	mole	syndicate
caper	fingerprint	money	theft
CIA (Central	gang	morality	thief
Intelligence	gangster	motive	threat
Agency)	getaway	murder	trace
clandestine	G-man	overt	traitor
client	godfather	parole	trap
clue	government	payoff	trial
code	gun	police	vice
conflict	heist	prison	victim
conscience	henchman	private eye	witness
convict	hunch	public	witness protection
corpse	hustler	revolver	program
corruption	illegal		

Creating a Hero

DIRECTIONS: Think about some famous spies or detectives you have read about or watched in the movies or on TV. What were they like? What traits did they have? Create a spy or detective of your own. Complete this worksheet, and then write a description about your spy or detective.

1. What is the name of your spy or detective? _____

2. Describe his or her background. _____

   _____

   _____

   _____

   _____

   _____

3. Describe his or her personality. _____

   _____

   _____

   _____

   _____

   _____

   _____

4. Describe his or her physical traits. _____

   _____

   _____

   _____

   _____

   _____

   _____

36

Western Words

TEACHING SUGGESTIONS

The days of the Old West were unique in history. No other country can boast of having had an era that marks the spirit of the pioneers. Stories about the Old West—of marshals staring down gunslingers on dusty streets, of wagon trains rumbling across the empty plains, of settlers staking claim to the rich earth of the prairie—remain popular even in the modern era of computers and high technology.

Activity 1 – Worksheet 36, "Writing a Western"

OBJECTIVE: Students are to write a story set in the Old West.

PROCEDURE: Hand out copies of List 36 and review the words with your students. Ask them to think about stories they have read or watched about the Old West. Discuss some of the unique elements of this era in American history; for example, westward expansion, the hardy individualism of the pioneers, and the toil and suffering that came along with building a nation.

Hand out copies of Worksheet 36. Explain to your students that they are to complete the worksheet and then write a story that is set in the Old West.

Activity 2 – Going Back in Time

OBJECTIVE: Students are to imagine living in the Old West; they are to write an account of what life would have been like.

PROCEDURE: Distribute copies of List 36 and review the words with your students. Ask them to imagine living in the Old West. What kind of person would they be? Some suggestions include: a marshal, an outlaw, a settler, a trapper, a cowpuncher, a Native American, a dance hall girl, a prospector, a trail boss on a cattle drive, or a teenager traveling west with his or her parents. For this assignment, students are to write an account describing the life they would have if they lived in the Old West.

See List 29, "Words of Adventure and Romance."

Western Words

Stories of the Old West are uniquely American. They are a part of our heritage. Proof of their popularity is the great many books and movies that tell of this brief but exciting period in history. Following are words right out of the Old West.

ambush	desperado	marshal	scalp
arrow	draw	maverick	settlement
badge	dude	mountains	settler
badlands	fistfight	mule	sheriff
bandit	fists	mustang	shootout
blacksmith	fort	noose	six-gun
bluff	frontier	outlaw	six-shooter
boots	gamble	paleface	smoke signal
border	ghost town	palomino	sodbuster
bounty hunter	gold	pioneer	sombrero
brand	gold mine	plains	spur
bronco	gold rush	pony	squaw
buckboard	gringo	Pony Express	stagecoach
buffalo	gun	posse	stampede
buggy	gunfight	prairie	stirrup
bullet	gunslinger	prospector	strongbox
bushwhack	hang	ranch	tepee
cactus	herd	range	tin star
canyon	hitch	ranger	tomahawk
carriage	hitching post	rawhide	town
cattle	holdup	reservation	trail
cattle drive	holster	reward	trail boss
cavalry	hombre	rifle	trooper
corral	homesteader	rodeo	tumbleweed
courage	horse	rowdy	valley
cowboy	Indian	rustler	wagon
cowgirl	iron horse	saddle	wagon train
cowpoke	jail	saddle horn	wanted poster
cowpuncher	lance	saddle tramp	war chief
dead	lariat	sagebrush	war party
deputy	lasso	saloon	water trough
desert	lynch	savage	wound

Writing a Western

DIRECTIONS: Think of the Old West. What was it like? You might think of settlers, cowpokes, gunfights, wagon trains, and pioneers. Complete this worksheet and then write a story that takes place in the Old West.

1. Describe the setting of your story. _____

   _____

   _____

   _____

2. Describe your main characters. _____

   _____

   _____

   _____

   _____

3. Describe the main conflict. _____

   _____

   _____

   _____

   _____

4. Briefly describe the plot. _____

   _____

   _____

   _____

   _____

5. Describe the climax. _____

   _____

   _____

   _____

SECTION FOUR

LISTS AND ACTIVITIES FOR
Writing Style

Phrases of Alliteration

TEACHING SUGGESTIONS

Many elements blend together to create an effective writing style. One of these elements is alliteration, the use of two or more words in a phrase or sentence that contains the same beginning sounds. Alliteration can add freshness as well as emphasis to writing. Encourage your students to use alliteration to make their writing distinctive.

Activity 1 – Worksheet 37, "Personal Poetry"

OBJECTIVE: Students are to write a poem on a topic of their choice; they are to use at least three examples of alliteration in their poems.

PROCEDURE: Distribute copies of List 37 and review the examples of alliteration with your students. Explain that, for this assignment, they are to select a topic and write a poem from a personal perspective. Offer these suggestions: everyday life, school, nature, sports, or relaxation. Permit students to develop their poems as they prefer; for example, with or without rhyme and with or without a specific meter. Remind them that they must include at least three examples of alliteration.

Hand out copies of Worksheet 37. Explain that completing the worksheet first will help students develop ideas for their poems. Upon completion of the assignment, you might like to arrange time for a poetry reading session in which students can share their poems.

Activity 2 – A Big Storm

OBJECTIVE: Students are to write a descriptive account of a major storm they experienced; they are to use at least three alliterative phrases in their writing.

PROCEDURE: Distribute copies of List 37 and review the examples of alliteration with your students. Ask them to think of a time they experienced a major storm. They might have been caught outdoors in it, traveled through it, or simply waited for it to pass while they were safe in their homes. Students are to write a descriptive account of this event, including at least three examples of alliteration in their writing.

See List 40, "Figures of Speech."

Phrases of Alliteration

When a writer puts together two or more words that have the same beginning sounds, he or she is using alliteration. While the effective use of alliteration can add freshness and style to your writing, too much of it can be distracting to the reader and thus undermine your ideas. Following are several examples of alliteration.

The little girl received a *big, blue ball* for her *birthday.*

He *mixed* and *matched* his clothing.

Entering the *burning building,* the *firefighters* rushed to *find* the trapped occupants.

Brave and *bold,* the warrior approached the king.

She picked the *red, ripe* tomato.

He came up with a *simple solution* to his problem.

The cave was *deep, dark,* and *damp.*

The *crystal clear* sky was *beautiful* to *behold.*

The *salty* breeze of the *sea soothed* him.

The *pug*-nosed *puppy played* all morning.

The *audience applauded after* every song.

Upon blastoff, the *silvery* rocket *ship streaked skyward.*

The *deepest* part of the night is a time for *dark dreams.*

Her heart was *hard* and cold.

The *calls* and *cries* of the gulls filled the air.

Prancing playfully, the colt relished his freedom.

The *blaring* of the *buzzer* jolted him from his daydreams.

A *great* orb, the *golden* moon cast its light over the *glen.*

The *cute kitten crept* about the room.

Personal Poetry

DIRECTIONS: Alliteration is the use of two or more words containing the same beginning sound in a phrase or sentence. The effective use of alliteration can add freshness and emphasis to your writing.

Think of some subjects of personal interest. Some suggestions include sports, school, a part-time job, nature, or simply hanging out with friends. Answer the questions below and write a poem about your subject. Be sure to include at least three examples of alliteration.

1. What is your topic? _____

_____

2. Why did you choose this topic? _____

_____

_____

_____

_____

_____

3. Describe the topic. _____

_____

_____

_____

_____

_____

_____

4. Write at least three examples of alliteration that relate to your topic. _____

_____

_____

_____

_____

_____

_____

38

Clichés

TEACHING SUGGESTIONS

Clichés are expressions that have been used countless times in countless stories and have long ago lost their freshness and excitement. They weaken writing by stealing its appeal and originality.

Students should be aware of clichés and understand that writing riddled with trite, hackneyed, or familiar expressions is at best mediocre. Fortunately, most clichés can be easily corrected. Many can simply be eliminated, while others can be rewritten.

Activity 1 – Worksheet 38, "The Major Mix-up"

OBJECTIVE: Students will revise clichés in a story.

PROCEDURE: Hand out copies of List 38 and review the examples of clichés with your students. Note that clichés are overused expressions that should always be revised, and point out that many of the examples on the list will be familiar.

For the activity, pass out copies of Worksheet 38. Instruct your students to identify the clichés, then rewrite the story, revising the clichés.

ANSWER KEY: Following is a list of clichés that appear in the story. Accept any reasonable revisions of *beyond a shadow of a doubt, on the other hand, always there when you really needed her, always willing to help, few and far between, simple solution, one in a million,* and *ripe old age.*

Activity 2 – "Mistakes Parents Make and What Can Be Done About Them"

OBJECTIVE: Students are to write an essay entitled "Mistakes Parents Make and What Can Be Done About Them," then proofread their stories to revise any clichés that they may have inadvertently used.

PROCEDURE: Distribute copies of List 38 to your students and review the examples of clichés. Next, ask your students to raise their hands if they feel their parents are perfect. Obviously, no one is perfect; we all make mistakes.

Now ask your students to think about mistakes their parents make in their interactions with them. Some mistakes students might think of include: not giving children a chance to explain their actions, feeling that children are too young or inexperienced to make decisions, or not trusting children.

For the activity, students are to write an essay about "Mistakes Parents Make and What Can Be Done About Them." Emphasize that an important part of the essay is addressing how parents can be helped to realize these mistakes, and thereby build a better relationship with their kids. After completion of their drafts, students should revise their work carefully, and especially revise any clichés that might have slipped into their writing.

See List 39, "Idioms," and List 41, "Jargon."

Clichés

Clichés, sometimes called trite expressions, are wasted phrases. They have become familiar and grown stale through too frequent use. They make writing dull and weaken style. Most clichés can be rewritten in a straightforward manner such as the following:

at death's door – near death
in this day and age – today
hale and hearty – robust

Following are some examples of clichés. It is likely that many of them will be familiar, and it is for this reason that you should try to keep them out of your writing.

accidents will happen	green with envy
always there when needed	grinning from ear to ear
always willing to help	hale and hearty
at death's door	haunted house
beautiful but dumb	heart in his (her) throat
beyond a shadow of a doubt	heart skipped a beat
blushing bride	impossible situation
broken into a million pieces	in a jiffy
budding genius	in no time
clouds of dust	in no uncertain terms
crystal clear	in record time
depths of despair	in this day and age
discreet silence	ivory tower
doomed to disappointment	last but not least
each and every	long arm of the law
eagle eye	make a long story short
easier said than done	my lips are sealed
eternal triangle	needles and pins
evil genius	no sooner said than done
evil magician	on the other hand
fair and square	one in a million
few and far between	ripe old age
flying saucer	rock-bottom prices
fond parents	sadder but wiser

Clichés *(continued)*

shiver down his (her) spine

sigh of relief

silence reigned

simple solution

supreme sacrifice

sweating bullets

tall, dark, and handsome

to the bitter end

trials and tribulations

unending sorrow

view with alarm

viselike grip

weary bones

when all is said and done

wicked witch

with all his might

word to the wise

wrinkled like a prune

The Major Mix-up

DIRECTIONS: Clichés are phrases that have been used so often in writing that they are familiar to readers. They weaken writing with their staleness. Identify the clichés in the story. Then rewrite the story, revising the clichés.

Jennifer looked impatiently at her watch. Her best friend, Dawn, was late again. Jennifer was sure beyond a shadow of a doubt that Dawn had forgotten that they were supposed to go to the movies. She tried to call Dawn at home, but the phone was busy, and Dawn's cell phone was turned off. Now Jennifer had nothing to do.

The more she thought about it, the madder Jennifer became. She decided that she and Dawn were finished being friends.

On the other hand, Jennifer thought, Dawn was always there when you really needed her. She was always willing to help whenever someone had a problem. In fact, friends like Dawn were few and far between.

When the phone rang, Jennifer hurried to answer it.

"Dawn, where are you?" she said testily.

When Dawn explained that she had been helping her sister with her homework and that her mother had been on the phone, Jennifer felt ashamed.

"Well, why don't we try to make the second show?" Jennifer asked, feeling that this was a simple solution. She was glad that Dawn agreed. Dawn was one in a million.

As she waited for Dawn to come, Jennifer smiled, thinking that they would probably be friends until ripe old age.

Idioms

TEACHING SUGGESTIONS

Idioms are common expressions that arise as language evolves. They cannot be taken literally. To "blow off steam" does not mean that one releases actual steam, but rather lets go of anger or tension. Most idioms need to be understood as having a separate meaning. While they are acceptable in informal conversation, under most circumstances they should be avoided in writing and speaking.

Activity 1 – Worksheet 39, "The Surprise Party"

OBJECTIVE: Students are to identify the idioms in a story; they are to determine the meaning of each idiom.

PROCEDURE: Hand out copies of List 39 and review the examples of idioms with your students. Explain that idioms are phrases that over time have taken on a separate meaning. Go over the examples and have volunteers explain the meanings of some of the idioms.

Distribute copies of Worksheet 39. Instruct your students to first identify the idioms, then write the meaning of each idiom on a separate sheet of paper.

ANSWER KEY: Following are the idioms in the story with their meanings. Accept any reasonable answers.

go all out – try hard

started the ball rolling – began

let the cat out of the bag – reveal the surprise

no-shows – people who don't come

sweating bullets – worrying

in the bag – a success

dead in his tracks – stopped

Activity 2 – Conducting an Idiom Scavenger Hunt

OBJECTIVE: Students are to find examples of idioms in everyday life.

PROCEDURE: This activity should be assigned over the course of a few days. You may prefer to have students work in pairs.

Begin the activity by handing out copies of List 39. Discuss the examples of idioms with your students, and note that idioms are common in everyday communication.

For the activity, students are to list as many examples of idioms they encounter as possible. Suggest that they might find idioms in the materials they read, in conversations, in the dialogue on TV shows and movies, and even on advertisements. They are to write down the idiom and the place in which they heard (or found) it.

At the end of the activity, allow time for students to share their lists of idioms. They will probably find that idioms are used far more commonly than they might have thought. Perhaps you can offer a prize of a homework pass to the students who find the most idioms.

See List 38, "Clichés," and List 41, "Jargon."

Idioms

Idioms are phrases that over time have assumed special meanings. For example, the idiom "got a tiger by the tail" does not mean that a person is actually holding onto a tiger, but rather that he or she has a big problem to solve. Because idioms are well-known phrases, much like clichés, they should be used sparingly in writing. Following are examples of idioms.

a ball of fire	know the ropes
add insult to injury	let the cat out of the bag
bark up the wrong tree	money talks
bend over backward	no-show
blow off steam	off his (her) rocker
by the skin of your teeth	on thin ice
call it a day	out of sight, out of mind
call onto the carpet	over the hill
carry a torch	pain in the neck
cough up the money	piece of cake
crack a smile	pulling his (her) leg
dead to the world	put on the dog
down in the dumps	put their heads together
drop a line	raining cats and dogs
face the music	red-carpet treatment
feel like a million bucks	rub him (her) the wrong way
feeling his (her) oats	sell like hotcakes
get the show on the road	shoot the breeze
go all out	spur of the moment
got a tiger by the tail	start the ball rolling
has a green thumb	stick together
has cold feet	still up in the air
hear through the grapevine	stop dead in his (her) tracks
hit the hay	sweat bullets
hit the spot	take a rain check
hold your horses	throw in the towel
hungry enough to eat a horse	up the creek without a paddle
in the bag	weigh a ton
in the same boat	wet behind the ears
jump down his (her) throat	writing on the wall

The Surprise Party

DIRECTIONS: Read the story and circle all the idioms. Then write the meaning of each one on the back of this sheet.

Sylvia and her mother had been planning the birthday party for her brother Raul for weeks. They intended to go all out and invite all of his friends. They started the ball rolling a month ago when they secretly mailed invitations to his friends. In the invitations, Sylvia cautioned people that the party was a surprise and that they should be careful not to let the cat out of the bag. Only a few people who did not respond yet might be no-shows.

On the night of the party, Sylvia had Jason, Raul's best friend, invite Raul to his house to watch a movie. But when Raul said he intended to begin work on his science project at home, Sylvia started sweating bullets. She did not know how to keep Raul from seeing the people arrive for his party. Fortunately, Jason convinced Raul that he could begin the science project tomorrow.

After everyone had arrived, Sylvia and her mother knew that the surprise was in the bag. A few moments later, Jason came with Raul.

When he stepped in the house and everyone yelled "Surprise!" Raul stopped dead in his tracks.

He was truly surprised.

40

Figures of Speech

TEACHING SUGGESTIONS

Figures of speech—metaphors, similes, and personification—can add powerful imagery to writing. Metaphors and similes make comparisons. Similes use the words *like, as,* or *than* to signal the comparison, while metaphors do not. Personification is a figure of speech in which nonhuman things are given human qualities.

Activity 1 – Worksheet 40, "An Enjoyable Day"

OBJECTIVE: Students are to think of an event they enjoyed and write an account of it; they are to include at least one example of a metaphor, a simile, and personification.

PROCEDURE: Distribute copies of List 40 and discuss the examples of figures of speech with your students. Ask them to think of an event they thoroughly enjoyed. It might have been a school dance, a football game, a camping trip, a party, or another event.

Hand out copies of Worksheet 40. Explain that students are to complete the worksheet, then write a descriptive account of this happy time. Encourage them to use figures of speech in their writing.

Activity 2 – Writing Nightmare Poems

OBJECTIVE: Students are to write a poem about a nightmare; they are to include at least one example each of a metaphor, a simile, and personification in their poems.

PROCEDURE: Hand out copies of List 40 and review the examples of figures of speech with your students. If you can obtain copies of scary or haunting poems (the work of Edgar Allan Poe is a good example), you might read a few to your students. This will help set the mood for the activity. To reduce any apprehension about writing poetry, leave the type of poetry up to your students. Poems can be either rhyming or nonrhyming and may or may not have a specific meter.

To begin the activity, ask your students to share their scariest nightmares. For the writing, encourage them to include at least one example of each figure of speech. At the end of the activity, you might want to compile a book of *Nightmare Poems.*

See List 37, "Phrases of Alliteration."

Figures of Speech

Authors can strengthen the power of their imagery through the skillful use of figures of speech.

SIMILES

Similes make comparisons using the words *like, as,* or *than.*

> His eyes flashed like lightning.
> The child climbed the tree as effortlessly as a monkey.
> She was tired but worked as smoothly as a robot.
> The wind howled like a wounded beast.
> The clouds were as gray as slate.
> He was meaner than a junkyard dog.

METAPHORS

Metaphors make implied comparisons. They *do not* use the words *like, as,* or *than.*

> He was a lion in war.
> The full moon, sun of the night, shone on his face.
> When he came to the chicken coop, the fox was a thief.
> Winter is a long, dark tunnel connecting summers.
> They were locked in a dark tomb of a cellar.

PERSONIFICATION

Personification is a figure of speech in which nonhuman things are given human qualities.

> Even the sky cried on the sorrowful day.
> The flower smiled at the sun.
> The mountains guarded the valley.
> The bird sang in happiness at the coming of spring.
> Circling the diver, the shark planned its attack.

An Enjoyable Day

DIRECTIONS: Think of an event that you found to be enjoyable. Complete the worksheet, then write an account of your "Enjoyable Day." Include at least one example each of a metaphor, a simile, and personification.

1. What was the event? _____
   _____
   _____

2. Where did it take place? _____
   _____
   _____

3. How did you get there? _____
   _____
   _____

4. Who was with you? _____
   _____
   _____

5. What was most memorable about this event? _____
   _____
   _____

6. Write one of each in relation to the event:

   Simile: _____
   _____

   Metaphor: _____
   _____

   Personification: _____
   _____

41

Jargon

TEACHING SUGGESTIONS

To be effective, communication must be clear. Perhaps the oldest rule remains the best rule: Keep it simple. As our society has become more complex, however, so has our language. A hundred years ago, phrases like lunar module, strategic arms, and Baby Boom had not been imagined by even the most astute visionaries. While the coining of new terms has given us the opportunity to communicate as never before, it has also allowed for greater confusion and misrepresentation.

Some people just don't like to communicate. Some try to impress others with their seeming command of language jawbreakers; others deliberately use milelong words and phrases to obscure ideas; still others believe that their convoluted writing and speaking is good. All of these people, whatever their reason, dabble in jargon.

The phrases of List 41 have actually been used in business, government, and education. Clearly, they, and similar examples, are not in the best interest of communication and should be avoided by writers and speakers.

Activity 1 – Worksheet 41, "Planning Your Future"

OBJECTIVE: Students are to identify examples of jargon in an article; they are then to rewrite the article, revising the jargon.

PROCEDURE: Distribute copies of List 41 to your students and review the examples of jargon. Explain that people may resort to jargon for a variety of reasons—they may want to confuse their listeners or readers, they may think that jargon adds to their stature, or they may simply not know how to communicate their ideas clearly. Whatever the reason, emphasize that jargon should always be avoided.

Hand out copies of Worksheet 41. For the assignment, students are to circle the phrases of jargon in the article and then rewrite the article, revising the jargon.

Following is a list of the phrases of jargon that appear in the article. While you should accept any reasonable revisions, possible revisions include:

> *the accumulated skills* – the skills
>
> *directive improvement* – discipline
>
> *goal-oriented member of society* – productive person
>
> *a human resource* – a worker
>
> *full-schedule human resource* – full-time worker
>
> *limited-schedule one* – part-time worker
>
> *incomplete success* – failure
>
> *philosophically disillusioned* – disappointed
>
> *advanced downward adjustments* – budget cuts
>
> *temporary work cessations* – layoffs
>
> *personal-directed improvements* – self-improvement
>
> *high-order position* – good job

Activity 2 – Having Fun with Jargon

OBJECTIVES: Students are to select a topic, generate a list of jargon relating to the topic, and write an account of their topic; they are to exchange their papers with a partner and try to determine the meanings of the jargon.

PROCEDURE: Hand out copies of List 41 and review the examples of jargon with your students. Discuss what jargon is and why it should be avoided.

Next, ask your students to select a topic—school, sports, dating, and part-time jobs are some ideas—and generate a list of doublespeak phrases that relate to the topic. After they have generated their lists, instruct them to write an account about their topics, including their examples of jargon.

When they are finished writing, they are to exchange their work with a friend and find each other's examples of jargon. Students should then discuss how they could revise their writing to eliminate any jargon.

See List 38, "Clichés," List 39, "Idioms," and List 42, "Overblown (Redundant) Phrases."

Jargon

Language that is not clear is ineffective; it does not communicate ideas. Sometimes, however, speakers and writers forget that simple fact and try instead to express themselves using big words and sentences. Other writers and speakers deliberately express their ideas in complex and confusing fashion because they may not want people to know what they are talking about. (This is a favorite tactic of some politicians.) Then there are people who believe that others will consider them smart if they use the biggest words they can find. All of these individuals are guilty of using jargon.

The phrases of the following list have actually been used by people in business, government, and education. You should always avoid jargon in speaking and writing, so beware of terms like these.

JARGON	INTERPRETATION
administrative aide	secretary
advanced downward adjustment	budget cut
advisory representative	salesperson
aerodynamic personnel decelerator	a parachute
career associate scanning professional	store checkout clerk
digital fever computer	a thermometer
directive improvement	discipline
downsizing personnel	a layoff
engine redesigner	mechanic
experienced vehicle	a used car
extended price	a higher price
fiscally disadvantaged	a poor person
food-service operation	restaurant
frame-supported tension structure	a tent
health care delivery system	medical services
housing units	apartments
human resources	employees
incomplete success	failure
jettison employees	fire people
limited-schedule human resource	part-time employee
metal cylinder storage container	a tin can
misinformation	a lie
misleading information	a lie

Jargon *(continued)*

JARGON	INTERPRETATION
nail technician	manicurist
non-goal-oriented member of society	a vagrant
pavement deficiency	pothole
philosophically disillusioned	disappointed
portable hand-held communications inscriber	a pencil
pre-owned vehicle	a used car
pressure garment assembly	spacesuit
safety-related event	accident
security coordinator	a bodyguard
service technician	repairperson
social expression product	a greeting card
strategic decision	a big decision
study skills areas	subjects
temporary work cessation	a layoff
therapeutic misadventure	malpractice
time frame	period
unauthorized withdrawal	bank robbery
uncontrolled contact with the ground	airplane crash
value added	benefit
visiting teacher	truant officer
well-behaved price	stable price
wooden interdental stimulator	toothpick

Planning Your Future

DIRECTIONS: Jargon is a term given to communication that clouds meaning and confuses the reader. Jargon is communication at its poorest.

Read the article and circle the examples of jargon. Then rewrite the article and revise the jargon, making the article clear.

It is important to plan your future. Only in that way can you hope to make a proper career choice in view of the accumulated skills you have attained. By planning effectively and maintaining a program of directive improvement, you will become a goal-oriented member of society.

Of course, you will be a human resource no matter what job you eventually secure. This will be true whether you are a full-schedule human resource or a limited-schedule one. Whatever you do, it is expected that you will avoid any instances of incomplete success.

In your search for a job, you may at times become philosophically disillusioned. Jobs are hard to find, especially during times when companies are forced to make advanced downward adjustments that may result in temporary work cessations.

However, through personal-directed improvements and patience, it is likely that you will find a high-order position.

Overblown (Redundant) Phrases

TEACHING SUGGESTIONS

Overblown phrases are phrases in which several words are used when one or two will suffice. Sometimes the same idea is repeated in an overblown phrase, making it redundant. A good example is *basic fundamentals*. *Basic* and *fundamentals* have similar meanings; the use of one of the words is sufficient. Overblown phrases are instances of overwriting. They clutter writing and obscure ideas, and they should be avoided.

Activity 1 – Worksheet 42, "The Big Test"

OBJECTIVES: Students are to identify the overblown phrases in a story; they are to rewrite the story, revising the overblown phrases.

PROCEDURE: Hand out copies of List 42 and review the overblown phrases with your students. Note how they are wordy or redundant, and emphasize the importance of concise writing.

Distribute copies of Worksheet 42. Explain that, for this activity, students are to identify the overblown phrases in the story, then rewrite the story, revising the overblown phrases. Upon completion of the activity, discuss how much tighter and smoother the revised stories are.

ANSWER KEY: Following is a list of overblown phrases that appear in the story. While you should accept all reasonable revisions, some possible revisions include:

> *biggest in size* – biggest
> *honest truth* – truth
> *absolutely necessary* – necessary
> *resulting effects* – effects
> *all of a sudden* – suddenly

postpone [the test] until later – postpone

prior to today – previously

past experience – experience

on the subject of history – history

serious danger – danger

heartbreaking tragedy – tragedy

totally destroyed – destroyed

think to myself – think

Activity 2 – Creating Images

OBJECTIVE: Students are to imagine a person they would like to be and write a descriptive account of this individual.

PROCEDURE: Distribute copies of List 42 and review the examples of overblown phrases with your students. For the assignment, ask your students to think of their personalities. What type of people are they? Suggest that they list at least five of their most prominent traits. If they could change any of these traits, which ones would they change? Why?

Instruct your students to write an account of the person they would like to be. (For students who say they would not change anything about themselves, suggest they write a description of themselves and explain why they would not want to change.) Encourage students to proofread their work carefully and make sure that they haven't used any overblown phrases.

See List 38, "Clichés," List 39, "Idioms," and List 41, "Jargon."

Overblown (Redundant) Phrases

Some authors muddle their writing with overblown, stuffy phrases in which they add unnecessary words or repeat ideas. Such phrases undermine the writer's purpose, which is to communicate. You should eliminate any excess words or phrases from your writing. The following list offers some overblown phrases that are regularly found in writing, as well as some simple ways to correct them.

OVERBLOWN PHRASE	CORRECTION
all of a sudden	suddenly
as a matter of fact	the fact is
as of this writing	yet
as to whether	whether
as yet	yet
at the present time	now, at present
basic fundamentals	fundamentals
be in a position to	can
be kind enough	please
big in size	big
by means of	by, with
climb up	climb
commute back and forth	commute
completely filled	filled
doctor by profession	doctor
due to the fact that	because
during the time that	while
each and every	every
end result	result
exactly the same	the same, identical
exact replica	replica
extreme hazard	hazard
foreign imports	imports
for the purpose of	to
in accordance with	by, with
in order to	to
in reference to	about

in regards to	as regards
in relation to	about
in the event that	if
in view of the fact	as
kindly arrange to send	please send
new record	record
none at all	none
on a few occasions	occasionally
on the subject of	about
order up	order
past history	past
personal friend	friend
postponed until later	postponed
prior to the start of	before
red in color	red
referred to as	called
resulting effects	effects
return back	return
seems to be	is
serious danger	danger
still persists	persists
successfully completed	completed
ten in number	ten
that there	that
the honest truth	truth
this here	this
thought to him- or herself	thought
totally destroyed	destroyed
totally unanimous	unanimous
under the circumstances	because
until such time	when
whether or not	whether
with regard to	about
with the exception of	except

The Big Test

DIRECTIONS: Read the story below and circle the overblown (redundant) phrases. After identifying these phrases, rewrite the story and revise these phrases.

As I walked into the classroom, I expected that the history test scheduled for today was the biggest in size that I ever took. And it was the most important of my life. The honest truth was that it was absolutely necessary for me to get a passing grade if I was to pass the course this quarter. If I failed, the resulting effects would ground me for six months!

All of a sudden, hoped filled me. What if Mrs. Wilson decided to postpone the test until later. Prior to today, she did that once, but my hopes crashed the moment she took the tests out of her briefcase.

As I sat there and watched Mrs. Wilson pass out the tests, I wished that I had studied. My past experience in taking tests on the subject of history was not good. If the past was any guideline for the present, I was in serious danger and I was headed for heartbreaking tragedy. My social life would be totally destroyed.

I began to think to myself what I would do if I was grounded for six months. The first thought that came to mind wasn't a happy one—I'd have plenty of time to study my history book!

43

Sequential Words and Phrases

TEACHING SUGGESTIONS

Sequential words and phrases serve several functions. Authors use them to organize information, rank information in order of importance, and indicate chronology. Sequential words and phrases help clarify writing.

Activity 1 – Worksheet 43, "A Great Responsibility"

OBJECTIVE: Students are to write an account describing a responsibility they have.

PROCEDURE: Hand out copies of List 43 and review the sequential words and phrases with your students. Explain that sequence, or ordering, is vital to writing. In an effective piece of writing, a logical sequence progresses from beginning to end. The proper use of sequential words and phrases will help ensure that the sequence of ideas is correct.

Distribute copies of Worksheet 43. For the assignment, instruct your students to complete the worksheet and write an account about an important responsibility they have. Encourage them to use sequential words and phrases in their writing.

Activity 2 – Follow My Directions

OBJECTIVE: Students are to select a place they know and write directions explaining how their friends can find this place.

PROCEDURE: Distribute copies of List 43 and review the sequential words and phrases with your students. To begin this activity, ask your students to select a place they visit—the beach, a park, a restaurant, a library, or similar spot. Starting from their home, they are to write directions explaining to a friend how to get to this destination.

See List 44, "Transitional Words and Phrases."

Sequential Words and Phrases

Sequential words and phrases are critical to good writing. They help clarify material for the reader by organizing information, indicating that more information is to come, ranking information in importance, or indicating time order. Following are words and phrases of sequence.

a few	first	now
additionally	following	on time
after	further	presently
aftermath	furthermore	previously
afterward	immediately	prior to
always	in addition	second
another	in conclusion	simultaneously
as soon as	in the first place	since
at once	interim	start
at the same time	last	subsequently
before	later	then
beforehand	latter	thereafter
begin	meanwhile	third
during	more	until
earlier	moreover	when
finally	next	while

A Great Responsibility

DIRECTIONS: Authors can help ensure that their writing is organized by using sequential words and phrases. Think of a responsibility you have—maybe a household or yard chore, achieving good grades in school, working at a part-time job, watching younger brothers and sisters, or a similar responsibility.

  Answer the questions on this worksheet, then write an account describing your great responsibility. Be sure to use sequential words and phrases in your writing.

1. What is your responsibility? _____

   _____

   _____

   _____

   _____

2. What are you required to do? _____

   _____

   _____

   _____

   _____

   _____

3. How do you feel about your responsibility? _____

   _____

   _____

   _____

   _____

4. How do you think others feel about the way you carry out your responsibility?

   _____

   _____

   _____

   _____

Transitional Words and Phrases

TEACHING SUGGESTIONS

Transitions are words and phrases that link ideas and make writing flow smoothly. They are essential for effective writing. Transitions may connect ideas within paragraphs, link paragraphs, or bridge one scene of a story or article to the next.

Activity 1 – Worksheet 44, "Highlights"

OBJECTIVE: Students are to select a time in their lives and write an account of the important events that occurred.

PROCEDURE: Distribute copies of List 44 and review the transitional words and phrases with your students. Explain the importance of transitions and emphasize that transitions serve as links between ideas. Without effective transitions, writing is rough and choppy.

Hand out copies of Worksheet 44 and instruct your students to select a time: last week, last month, or even some period of last year. Ask them to think of the highlights of that period. What important events occurred? Completing the worksheet first will help students to organize their ideas. Encourage them to concentrate on using effective transitions in their writing.

Activity 2 – "Why Students Succeed (or Fail)"

OBJECTIVE: Students are to choose either of the topics "Why Students Succeed" or "Why Students Fail" and write an essay.

PROCEDURE: Hand out copies of List 44 and review the transitional words and phrases with your students. Briefly discuss the importance of transitions. For this assignment, ask your students to select either of the given topics. You might wish to discuss the topics first to stimulate ideas.

Instruct your students to write an essay, explaining their thoughts on the topics. Encourage them to use effective transitions in their writing.

See List 43, "Sequential Words and Phrases."

Transitional Words and Phrases

Transitions are words, phrases, or sentences that link ideas in a paragraph or connect one paragraph to another. Sometimes transitions are used to link scenes of a story. They are crucial for smooth writing. Following are common transitional words and phrases.

above	despite	instead of
accordingly	different from	just as
additionally	due to	later
after	during	moreover
also	earlier	much as
although	even though	nevertheless
another	finally	next
as a result	first	on the other hand
at last	for example	outside
because	for instance	rather than
before	further	similarly
behind	furthermore	so
below	however	such
beside	in addition to	therefore
beyond	in fact	through
consequently	in spite of	thus
contrary to	inside	under

Highlights

DIRECTIONS: Authors use transitions to make their writing smooth. Think of a time—perhaps last week, last month, or a time of last year—and list the important events that occurred during this time. Next, write an account of these highlights. Be sure to use good transitions in your writing.

Highlight One: _____

_____

Details: _____

_____

_____

_____

_____

Highlight Two: _____

_____

Details: _____

_____

_____

_____

_____

Highlight Three: _____

_____

Details: _____

_____

_____

_____

_____

RULES, CHECKLISTS, AND ACTIVITIES FOR
Student Writers

45

Parts of Speech

TEACHING SUGGESTIONS

The English language contains about half a million words. All of these words can be grouped into eight parts of speech. Understanding these classifications can help students gain a greater appreciation and knowledge of English.

Activity 1 – Worksheet 45, "Finding All the Parts"

OBJECTIVE: Students will identify parts of speech in sentences.

PROCEDURE: Distribute copies of List 45 and review the parts of speech with your students. Emphasize that all words in English can be classified according to these eight categories. You might also mention that, depending on how a word is used in a sentence, it may fit into one of several categories.

Hand out copies of Worksheet 45. For the activity, students are to identify words according to their part of speech. They are to write the words on the lines after their designations.

ANSWER KEY: 1. *nouns:* Martina, sports, soccer; *verbs:* enjoys, is.   2. *verb:* approached; *prepositions:* from, with.   3. *pronouns:* they, their; *verbs:* left, took.   4. *verb:* went; *prepositions:* to, with.   5. *nouns:* rain, night, drought; *adjectives:* heavy, last, the. 6. *noun:* Tom; *adverb:* when.   7. *verbs:* cried, pulled; *interjection:* Look out. 8. *adverbs:* swiftly, quietly; *conjunction:* and.   9. *pronouns:* she, her; *adverb:* carefully.   10. *nouns:* Tom, Jim, things, music; *conjunctions:* and, but.

Activity 2 – "Cyber World"

OBJECTIVES: Students are to write an essay in which they discuss the value (or lack of value) of the Internet. Upon completion of their essays, they are to review their work and identify at least three examples of all parts of speech, except interjections (unless, of course, they wrote an extremely emotional essay).

PROCEDURE: Distribute copies of List 45 and review the parts of speech with your students. Explain that, as civilization advances, new ideas bring with them new words. These words are assimilated into our language. A generation ago, the Internet was in its earliest stages, used mostly by the academic and military establishments. Now millions of Americans visit cyberspace every day to send e-mail, chat online, find information, shop, or simply browse. The Internet has given rise to an entire vocabulary.

For the activity, students are to write an essay explaining what they feel is the value, or lack of value, of the Internet. Remind them that, upon completion of their writing, they are to identify three examples of each part of speech, except interjections.

See List 46, "Sentences, Fragments, and Run-ons," List 50, "Irregular Verb Forms," List 52, "Major Categories of Pronouns," and List 53, "Common Prepositions."

Parts of Speech

All of the words in the English language can be classified according to eight parts of speech. Depending on how they are used in a sentence, some words can fall into various categories. Following are the parts of speech and some examples.

- **Noun:** A noun is a word that names a person, place, thing, or idea. Nouns may be *common* or *proper*. *Common nouns* name any person, place, thing, or idea, while *proper nouns* are specific and must always be capitalized.

  Examples of Common Nouns: child, valley, table, truth.

  Examples of Proper Nouns: Jennifer, Texas, the George Washington Bridge, Equal Rights

- **Verb:** A verb is a word that shows action, a condition, or state of being.

  Examples: walk, watched, enjoy, study, imagine, am, is, was, were, remains, finish, missed

- **Pronoun:** A pronoun is a word that is used in place of a noun.

  Examples: I, you, he, she, it, we, you, they, him, her, them, mine, our, someone, who, whom, whose

- **Adjective:** An adjective is a word that is used to describe a noun or pronoun. A *proper adjective* is an adjective that is formed from a proper noun. It must always be capitalized.

  Examples: big, small, tall, short, blue, long, English, German, Mexican, Spanish, Chinese, African

- **Adverb:** An adverb is a word that is used to describe a verb, an adjective, or another adverb.

  Examples: silently, quietly, swiftly, always, seldom, often, never, very

- **Conjunction:** A conjunction is a word that is used to join words or groups of words.

  Examples: and, or, but, nor, either, neither, because, however, since

- **Preposition:** A preposition is a word that is used to show the relationship of a noun or pronoun to another word.

  Examples: above, at, below, for, of, from, to, during, after

- **Interjection:** An interjection is a word or phrase that is used to express strong emotion.

  Examples: Oh! Oh no! Look out! Great! Aha!

Finding All the Parts

DIRECTIONS: Identify the required parts of speech in each sentence. Write the words in the spaces after the sentences.

1. Martina enjoys several sports, but her favorite is soccer.

   nouns:_____   verbs:_____

2. The storm approached from the south with hail and heavy rain.

   verb:_____   prepositions:_____

3. Before the Millers left for vacation, they took their dog to the kennel.

   pronouns:_____   verbs:_____

4. Tara went to the movies with friends yesterday.

   verb:_____   prepositions:_____

5. Heavy rain last night helped to ease the drought.

   nouns:_____   adjectives:_____

6. Tom asked, "When will we leave?"

   noun:_____   adverb:_____

7. "Look out!" cried Nan as she pulled Tasha out of the path of the speeding car.

   verbs:_____   interjection:_____

8. The fox ran swiftly and quietly toward the henhouse.

   adverbs:_____   conjunction:_____

9. She retraced her steps carefully in hopes of finding the lost wallet.

   pronouns:_____   adverb:_____

10. Tom and Jim agree on most things, but they like different music.

   nouns:_____   conjunctions:_____

Sentences, Fragments, and Run-ons

TEACHING SUGGESTIONS

Sentences are the foundation of written and spoken English. A sentence expresses a complete thought and facilitates the sharing of ideas. Students need to understand the importance of complete sentences to writing and speaking.

Activity 1 – Worksheet 46, "The Decision"

OBJECTIVES: Students are to identify fragments and run-ons in a story; they are to rewrite the story, correcting the fragments and run-ons.

PROCEDURE: Distribute copies of List 46 and discuss the examples of complete sentences, fragments, and run-ons. Explain that to be complete a sentence must have a subject and predicate. A subject and predicate express a complete thought.

Hand out copies of Worksheet 46. Explain that fragments make writing choppy, while run-ons crowd information and obscure ideas. For the activity, students are to identify and revise fragments and run-ons.

ANSWER KEY: Following are the fragments and run-ons. Accept reasonable revisions. *Run-on:* I could keep working part-time at the animal hospital, I could quit and work with my best friend, Samantha, at the clothing shop at the mall, we could have a lot of fun. *Fragment:* The toughest decision of my life. *Run-on:* The pay was a little less, I would receive a discount on any clothes I bought at the store. *Fragment:* A great incentive. *Fragment:* A lot of hours.

Activity 2 – An Admirable Profession

OBJECTIVE: Students are to write an account of a profession they feel is admirable.

PROCEDURE: Hand out copies of List 46 and review the examples of sentences, fragments, and run-ons with your students. Note that fragments and run-ons disrupt the flow of ideas and undermine communication.

For the activity, your students are to write a description of a profession they feel is worthy of respect. In their accounts, suggest that they focus on why the profession they chose is important and how it benefits others. Encourage your students to proofread their work carefully and revise any instances of fragments or run-ons.

Sentences, Fragments, and Run-ons

Complete sentences are the foundation of written and spoken English, for they contain a subject and predicate and express a complete thought. Following are three types of sentences and two common types of mistakes people make when writing.

- A *simple sentence* may be one of four kinds.

  Declarative: It snowed all night.

  Interrogative: Where did I leave my coat?

  Imperative: Please close the window.

  Exclamatory: Look out!

- A *compound sentence* contains two sentences joined by a comma and the conjunctions *and, but, or,* or *nor.*

  Sylvia likes to listen to jazz, but her sister prefers rock and roll.

- A *complex sentence* contains a main clause and one or more subordinate clauses.

  Because of the blizzard, all flights to Denver were delayed indefinitely.

- A *fragment* is an incomplete thought. Fragments should always be corrected.

  A walk in the park. (fragment)

  Yesterday I took a walk in the park. (correct)

- A *run-on* is two or more sentences strung together without proper punctuation. Run-ons can be corrected by writing the two sentences separately or by joining the two sentences with a comma and a word such as *and, but, or,* or *nor.*

  Chris finished his homework, he started his science project before dinner. (run-on)

  Chris finished his homework, and he started his science project before dinner. (correct)

The Decision

DIRECTIONS: Identify the examples of fragments and run-ons in the story. Rewrite and revise the story, correcting the fragments and run-ons.

It was a tough decision. I could keep working part-time at the animal hospital, I could quit and work with my best friend, Samantha, at the clothing shop at the mall, we could have a lot of fun. The toughest decision of my life.

I tried to consider all the factors. I enjoyed working at the animal hospital. I like animals and hope to be a veterinarian someday. The pay at the hospital was good, and the director allowed me to work two days a week after school and on Saturday. The hours fit my schedule.

Working at the clothing shop had advantages, too. The pay was a little less, I would receive a discount on any clothes I bought at the store. A great incentive. But the hours weren't as good. I would have to work three days a week after school, and every other Saturday and Sunday. A lot of hours. I was afraid the longer hours might affect my schoolwork.

The more I thought about it, I realized the decision wasn't hard at all. I kept working at the animal hospital. Not only did I like helping animals, but my experience there is important to my goal of becoming a veterinarian.

Rules for Capitalization

TEACHING SUGGESTIONS

By middle school, most students should have a solid understanding of the rules for capitalization. An occasional review, however, is usually helpful.

Activity 1 – Worksheet 47, "A Capital Idea"

OBJECTIVE: Students are to correct capital letters in sentences.

PROCEDURE: Distribute copies of Worksheet 47 and review the rules for capitalization with your students. Explain that correct writing requires an understanding of capitalization. (This is more important than ever with the proliferation of e-mail and chat rooms, and with writers trying to compose with ever greater speed, often ignoring conventional grammar and punctuation. Such habits can slip into other forms of writing.)

Hand out copies of Worksheet 47. Instruct your students to rewrite the sentences on a separate sheet of paper, correcting the necessary capital letters.

ANSWER KEY: 1. The Thomases stayed in a water-front apartment in San Juan during their vacation. 2. Bekka read *To Kill a Mockingbird* for her book review. 3. A snow-storm left eight inches of snow across the valley last night. 4. Tina decided to invite her friends to a pool party on June 21 to celebrate the end of the school year. 5. On Monday, Mr. Simon assigned a science project. 6. Carlos just moved into town and now lives at 324 Willis Avenue. 7. The little girl named the kitten Sunshine because of its golden fur. 8. Todd mailed the package to P.O. Box 145, Centerville, NY. 9. Casey and her parents visited the Museum of Natural History during their trip to New York City. 10. The Amazon River is by far the longest river in South America. 11. The captain of the town's police department led a panel discussion on school safety. 12. Our class has students whose families came from Europe, South America, Africa, and Asia.

Activity 2 – Writing About an Imaginary Pet

OBJECTIVES: Students are to write an account of an imaginary pet; they are to carefully proofread and correct any errors in capitalization.

PROCEDURE: Hand out copies of List 47 and review the rules for capitalization with your students. Emphasize that capital letters are essential to writing, because they signal the start of sentences, identify proper nouns and proper adjectives, help to indicate titles, and are used with abbreviations and acronyms.

For this activity, your students are to write an account of an imaginary pet. Since the pet is imaginary, it can be "invented," using traits of various animals. In their accounts, suggest that students describe their pets, where they would obtain these pets, and why these "imaginary" pets would be unique. Remind your students to proofread carefully and especially to correct capitalization.

See List 48, "Rules for Punctuation."

Rules for Capitalization

The following rules for capitalization are necessary for written communication.

- Capitalize proper nouns and proper adjectives. *Examples:* George Washington, the Golden Gate Bridge, Mexican food

- Capitalize the pronoun I.

- Capitalize initials. *Examples:* John F. Kennedy, Ursula K. Le Guin, J.K. Rowling

- Capitalize titles when they are attached to a name. *Examples:* Doctor Jones, General Smith, Aunt Janet, Pastor Wallace

- Capitalize the first word in a sentence and the first word in a quotation. *Example:* In a disappointed voice, Tom said, "The game is postponed."

- Capitalize the names of cities, states, countries, and continents. *Examples:* Philadelphia, Texas, United States of America, Africa

- Capitalize the names of rivers, oceans, mountains, and other geographical sites. *Examples:* Mississippi River, Pacific Ocean, Rocky Mountains, the Oregon Trail

- Capitalize the days of the week, months of the year, public and religious holidays. *Examples:* Sunday, January, Fourth of July, Christmas, Yom Kippur, Ramadan

- Capitalize the names of streets and avenues. *Examples:* Main Street, Sunrise Avenue, Rabbit Court, Jackson Road

- Capitalize the names of companies, organizations, and clubs. *Examples:* General Motors, the Federal Bureau of Investigation (FBI), the Riverside Joggers Club

- Capitalize the first word and all important words in the titles of books, newspapers, magazines, poems, songs, movies, plays, and works of art. *Examples: Call of the Wild* (book), the Mona Lisa

- Capitalize all letters of acronyms and most abbreviations. *Examples:* NATO, U.S.A., P.O. Box

- Capitalize all of the words of the greeting of a letter. Only capitalize the first word of the closing of a letter. *Examples:* Dear Miss Simmons, Yours truly,

A Capital Idea

DIRECTIONS: Rewrite the sentences in the spaces provided, correcting the mistakes in capitalization.

1. The Thomases stayed in a Water-front apartment in san Juan during their vacation.

2. Bekka read *To Kill A Mockingbird* for her Book Review.

3. a snowstorm left eight inches of snow across the Valley last night.

4. Tina decided to invite her friends to a Pool Party on june 21 to celebrate the end of the School Year.

5. On monday, mr. Simon assigned a Science project.

6. Carlos just moved into Town and now lives at 324 Willis avenue.

7. the little girl named the kitten sunshine because of its golden fur.

8. Todd mailed the package to p.o. box 145, Centerville, NY.

9. Casey and her parents visited the museum of natural history during their trip to New York city.

10. The Amazon river is by far the longest river in south America.

11. The captain of the town's Police Department led a panel discussion on school safety.

12. Our class has students whose families came from Europe, south America, Africa, and Asia.

Rules for Punctuation

TEACHING SUGGESTIONS

Punctuation is the set of symbols that helps to clarify ideas in written material. Imagine trying to read the information on this page without punctuation. Once students learn to use punctuation correctly, their overall efforts at writing become easier. The rules of the accompanying list can help.

Activity 1 – Worksheet 48, "Punctuation Corrector"

OBJECTIVE: Students are to correct punctuation in a set of sentences.

PROCEDURE: Hand out copies of List 48 and review the punctuation rules with your students. Depending on the abilities of your students, you may find it beneficial to review the list in parts. Explain that punctuation helps a writer's ideas stand out. For example, at its simplest, punctuation cues a reader when a sentence begins and when it ends, highlights titles of books and stories, and sets off dialogue and quotations.

Pass out copies of Worksheet 48. Note that students are to rewrite the sentences with correct punctuation on a separate sheet of paper. Mention that, while some sentences might be missing punctuation, in others punctuation might be used incorrectly.

ANSWER KEY: 1. Last summer Sara and her sister visited their grandmother in Jacksonville, Florida.   2. Tom, Jason's brother, is ten years old.   3. "Is it supposed to rain tomorrow?" asked Reynaldo.   4. One of Casey's all-time favorite books is *Charlotte's Web* by E.B. White.   5. "Oh no!" Vince groaned when he realized he had left his science paper at home.   6. The Palmer City Environmental Society meets the last Thursday of each month in the town library at 7:00 P.M.   7. Although she enjoyed babysitting the Smith twins, Hannah was exhausted by the time they finally went to sleep.   8. Nan packed the picnic basket with sandwiches, cookies, juice, and fruits.   9. Leena, of course, loves every cat she sees.   10. "Let's go to the library after school on Wednesday," said Dan.   11. Dr. Steven Wilson, a local physician, presented an assembly on safety rules all students should know. 12. Stan couldn't remember where he left his keys.

Activity 2 – Writing Without Punctuation

OBJECTIVES: Students are to write a description of a topic of their choice without punctuation. They will exchange their writing with a classmate, then proofread and add the necessary punctuation to each other's writing.

PROCEDURE: Distribute copies of List 48 and review the rules for punctuation with your students. Emphasize the importance of punctuation to the overall communication of ideas.

Explain that for this activity, students are to write a description or account of a topic of their choice. However, they are to write without using punctuation. Upon completion of the writing, they will exchange papers with another student and provide the necessary punctuation to each other's papers. When the activity is done, conduct a discussion of students' impressions about the need for punctuation.

See List 47, "Rules for Capitalization."

Rules for Punctuation

The following rules for punctuation are critical for effective writing.

RULES FOR USING END MARKS

- Use a period:

    To end a declarative sentence (statement). *Example:* It is hot outside.

    After an imperative sentence (command). *Example:* Open the window.

    At the end of an abbreviation. *Examples:* Dr., Mrs., Mon., Feb.

    With initials. *Example:* S.E. Hinton

- Use a question mark after an interrogative sentence (question). *Example:* When does the show begin?

- Use an exclamation point after an exclamatory sentence (strong emotion). *Example:* Oh no!

USE COMMAS

- Between the words, phrases, and clauses in a series. *Example:* steak, potatoes, and corn

- Between the names of cities and states. *Example:* Los Angeles, California

- Between the day and year in dates. *Example:* July 4, 2004

- To set off nouns in direct address. *Example:* Lisa, it is time to leave.

- To indicate direct quotations in a sentence. *Example:* "The science projects are due Friday," said Ben.

- Before *and, but, or,* or *nor* in a compound sentence. *Example:* Santo wants to go to the shore for the family vacation, but his sister prefers the mountains.

- To set off an appositive. *Example:* Jamie, the new student, comes from Minnesota.

- After an introductory word, phrase, or clause in a sentence. *Example:* Frightened by the howling winds of the storm, the little girl couldn't sleep.

- To separate adjectives or adverbs of equal importance. *Example:* The plump, smiling fellow hardly looked like a powerful wizard.

- To set off parenthetical and nonessential expressions. *Example:* If any of our products are defective, of course, they will be replaced free of charge.

- After the greeting of a friendly letter and after the closing of all letters. *Examples:* Dear Bill, Yours truly,

- In numbers of more than three digits. *Example:* 24,687

Rules for Punctuation *(continued)*

USE A COLON

- To set off words in a list following an independent clause. *Example:* André packed the following for the ski trip: ski pants, a parka, sweaters, heavy socks, a ski hat, and warm gloves.

- Between hours and minutes. *Example:* 3:15 P.M.

- After the greeting of a business letter. *Example:* Dear Ms. Jones:

- To indicate an important idea. *Example:* Directions: Complete the worksheet.

USE A SEMICOLON

- Between independent clauses not joined by conjunctions. *Example:* Jon felt confident about the game; Eduardo did not.

- Between main clauses if there are commas in one or both of the clauses. *Example:* She finished the first part of the project easily; however, she had trouble with the second.

USE AN APOSTROPHE

- In contractions to show what letters are missing. *Examples:* cannot—can't, has not—hasn't

- To show possessive nouns. *Examples:* Jen's books, the twin sisters' bikes, Charles's car

USE QUOTATION MARKS

- To indicate the direct words of a speaker. *Example:* "I have no homework tonight," Rachel said.

- To indicate the titles of short stories, articles, songs, poems, or the titles of chapters in books. *Example:* "The Road Not Taken" (poem)

USE UNDERLINING (ITALICS)

- For the titles of books, movies, and works of art. *Example:* <u>The Outsiders</u> (book)

- For the names of newspapers, magazines, ships, trains, planes, and spacecraft. *Example:* <u>The New York Times</u> (newspaper)

- For words that require special emphasis. *Example:* There is a difference between <u>counsel</u> and <u>council</u>.

Rules for Punctuation *(continued)*

USE PARENTHESES

- To enclose information that is added to a sentence but is not of critical importance. *Example:* The chart (see page 3) has been updated.

USE HYPHENS

- To connect two or more words to form compound words. *Example:* up-to-date

- To divide words into syllables. *Example:* fol-low

- When writing certain numbers. *Examples:* forty-two, fifty-five, eighty-one

USE DASHES

- To signal breaks in thought. *Example:* Make a right after the gas station—it has a big flag in front—then turn onto Cedar Drive.

Punctuation Corrector

DIRECTIONS: Rewrite the following sentences with correct punctuation.

1. Last summer Sara, and her sister visited their grandmother in Jacksonville Florida.

   _____

2. Tom; Jasons brother, is ten years old.

   _____

3. "Is it supposed to rain tomorrow," asked Reynaldo?

   _____

4. One of Casey's all-time favorite books is "Charlotte's Web" by E.b. White.

   _____

5. "Oh no Vince groaned when he realized he had left his science paper at home."

   _____

6. The Palmer City Environmental Society meet's the last Thursday of each month in the
   town library at 7,00 P.M.

   _____

7. Although she enjoyed baby-sitting the Smith twins Hannah was exhausted, by the time
   they finally went to sleep.

   _____

8. Nan packed the picnic basket; with sandwiches, cookies, juice and, fruits.

   _____

9. Leena of course, loves every cat she sees.

   _____

10. "Lets go to the library after school on Wednesday" said Dan.

    _____

11. Dr Steven Wilson a local physician, presented an assembly on safety rules all students
    should know.

    _____

12. Stan couldnt remember where he left his keys?

    _____

THE WRITING TEACHER'S BOOK OF LISTS

49

Spelling Rules

TEACHING SUGGESTIONS

The ability to spell is a basic skill for writing. Although not every student can become a perfect speller, most can become competent spellers, particularly if they follow the guidelines of List 49.

Activity 1 – Worksheet 49, "A Spelling Challenge"

OBJECTIVE: Students are to complete a spelling quiz containing frequently misspelled words.

PROCEDURE: Distribute copies of List 49 and review the spelling rules with your students. Explain that English spelling rules reflect the richness of the language. Because English over the years has assimilated so many words from other languages, there are exceptions to just about every rule. Emphasize, however, that despite the exceptions, most students can become competent spellers. (You might also remind students to use spelling checkers when writing on computers and to refer to a dictionary whenever they are in doubt over the correct spelling of a word.)

Hand out copies of Worksheet 49. Explain that the worksheet is in the form of a spelling quiz containing words that are often misspelled. Encourage your students to concentrate while completing the quiz. When they are finished, you may find it beneficial to go over the answers orally.

ANSWER KEY: 1. believe 2. balance 3. extraordinary 4. courageous 5. cemetery 6. icicle 7. identical 8. boundary 9. wondrous 10. descend 11. boredom 12. surprise 13. incredible 14. February 15. favorable

Activity 2 – Creating Student-Generated Spelling Quizzes

OBJECTIVES: Students are to create spelling quizzes; they will exchange and complete quizzes with a partner.

PROCEDURE: Distribute copies of List 49 and review the spelling rules with your students. Also, depending on the abilities of your students, hand out copies of List 5, "Hard-to-Spell Words (Intermediate)," and List 6, "Hard-to-Spell Words (Advanced)." You may, of course, hand out copies of both lists, or you may prefer to create lists of words taken from your students' spelling, reading, science, or social studies programs.

For the activity, students are to create a spelling quiz similar to the quiz provided on Worksheet 49. After creating their quizzes (with answer keys), students are to exchange their quizzes with a classmate and complete each other's quiz. You might find this to be a useful activity throughout the year.

See List 5, "Hard-to-Spell Words (Intermediate)," and List 6, "Hard-to-Spell Words (Advanced)."

Spelling Rules

Following the spelling rules below can help you become a better speller. However, whenever in doubt, consult a dictionary.

1. For many words, **s** can be added without a spelling change. *Examples:* cat – cats, storm – storms, hill – hills

2. For words that end in **ch, s, sh, x,** or **z, es** can be added without a spelling change. *Examples:* church – churches, genius – geniuses, bush – bushes, box – boxes, buzz – buzzes

3. For words with **ie** and **ei:**
   - When the sound of a word is **e,** spell the word with **ie,** except after **c.** *Examples:* piece, relieve; examples *"except after c":* ceiling, perceive
   - When the sound of a word is not **e,** spell the word **ei,** especially if the sound is **a.** *Examples:* weight, sleigh
   - There are exceptions to the above. Examples: friend, either, weird

4. For most words ending in **f** or **fe:**
   - When adding **s** or **es,** change the **f** to **v,** then add **s** or **es.** *Examples:* wife – wives, knife – knives, thief – thieves
   - There are exceptions to the above. Examples: roof – roofs, chief – chiefs

5. For most words ending in **o:**
   - If the **o** follows a vowel, add **s** to form the plural. *Examples:* radio – radios, rodeo – rodeos
   - If the **o** follows a consonant, add **es** to form the plural. *Examples:* hero – heroes, potato – potatoes

6. For most words ending in a consonant and **y,** change the **y** to **i** before an ending that does not begin with **i.** *Examples:* lady – ladies, try – tried

7. For most words ending in a vowel and **y,** keep the **y** when adding an ending. *Examples:* stay – stayed, employ – employing, turkey – turkeys

Spelling Rules *(continued)*

8. For most one-syllable words that end in one vowel and one consonant, double the consonant when adding an ending that starts with a vowel. *Examples:* thin – thinner, run – running, flat – flatter

9. For most two-syllable words that end in one vowel and one consonant, and the accent is on the second syllable, double the consonant when adding an ending that starts with a vowel. *Examples:* begin – beginning, refer – referred

10. Irregular nouns do not follow spelling rules when changing from singular to plural.

    • Some irregular nouns change their forms. *Examples:* man – men, woman – women, child – children, mouse – mice, goose – geese

    • Some irregular nouns have the same spelling in the singular and plural forms. *Examples:* deer – deer, moose – moose, sheep – sheep

A Spelling Challenge

DIRECTIONS: Place a check before the word in each row that is spelled incorrectly.

1. ___ arrive   ___ beleive   ___ rhyme   ___ disguise

2. ___ chapter   ___ distress   ___ napkin   ___ balence

3. ___ exterordinary   ___ momentum   ___ literacy   ___ decimal

4. ___ minimum   ___ esteem   ___ curageous   ___ persist

5. ___ career   ___ cemetary   ___ abrupt   ___ physical

6. ___ official   ___ isicle   ___ foreign   ___ bewilder

7. ___ identicle   ___ parallel   ___ disaster   ___ business

8. ___ leisure   ___ original   ___ boundery   ___ dependent

9. ___ government   ___ wonderous   ___ colossal   ___ perceive

10. ___ desend   ___ brilliant   ___ grateful   ___ furious

11. ___ receive   ___ knowledge   ___ ominous   ___ bordom

12. ___ nervous   ___ suprize   ___ imagination   ___ library

13. ___ detective   ___ magazine   ___ cavity   ___ incredable

14. ___ reluctant   ___ Febuary   ___ isle   ___ detergent

15. ___ gadget   ___ opportunity   ___ faverable   ___ recycle

50

Irregular Verbs

TEACHING SUGGESTIONS

Most verbs are *regular* verbs, meaning that they form their past tense by adding **d** or **ed.** Verbs that do not form their past tense in this manner are called *irregular* verbs. Because there are no rules for changing *irregular* verbs to the past and past participle forms, these verbs can cause much confusion.

Activity 1 – Worksheet 50, "And the Correct Verb Is . . ."

OBJECTIVE: Students are to complete sentences using the correct forms of irregular verbs.

PROCEDURE: Hand out copies of List 50 and review the irregular verbs with your students. If necessary, explain the differences between the past and past participle forms. Suggest to your students that they learn as many of these verbs as they can, and that they should always consult a dictionary or an author's guidebook when in doubt.

Distribute copies of Worksheet 50. Explain that students are to complete the sentences by writing the correct form of the irregular verbs in the blanks.

ANSWER KEY: 1. crept   2. taught   3. flown   4. seen   5. slew   6. swam   7. caught   8. written   9. known   10. frozen   11. burst   12. become

Activity 2 – Writing About Exceptions to the Ordinary

OBJECTIVE: Students are to write an account of a topic of their choice in which an exception to a rule or standard course of action is demonstrated.

PROCEDURE: Distribute copies of List 50 and review the irregular verbs with your students. Explain that, just as irregular verbs prove to be exceptions to the usual rules for forming the past and past participle forms of verbs, life is filled with instances of exceptions to the ordinary or commonplace. Ask your students to offer some examples, such as a female placekicker in football, the grandmother who returns to college to earn her degree, or the boy who as a child feared water but has overcome that fear to become a lifeguard.

For the activity, students are to write an account of an exception to the ordinary. Encourage them to proofread their work carefully and to pay close attention to any irregular verbs.

See List 51, "Verb Tenses."

Irregular Verbs

Most verbs form their past tense by adding **d** or **ed.** Verbs that do not form their past tense in this manner are called *irregular* verbs. The past participle of irregular verbs requires the use of the helping verbs *has, have,* or *had.* Following is a list of some of the most common irregular verbs.

PRESENT TENSE	PAST TENSE	PAST PARTICIPLE
bear	bore	has, have, had borne
beat	beat	has, have, had beaten
become	became	has, have, had become
begin	began	has, have, had begun
bite	bit	has, have, had bitten
blow	blew	has, have, had blown
break	broke	has, have, had broken
bring	brought	has, have, had brought
burst	burst	has, have, had burst
catch	caught	has, have, had caught
choose	chose	has, have, had chosen
come	came	has, have, had come
creep	crept	has, have, had crept
do	did	has, have, had done
draw	drew	has, have, had drawn
drink	drank	has, have, had drunk
drive	drove	has, have, had driven
eat	ate	has, have, had eaten
fall	fell	has, have, had fallen
fight	fought	has, have, had fought
flee	fled	has, have, had fled
fling	flung	has, have, had flung
fly	flew	has, have, had flown
freeze	froze	has, have, had frozen
give	gave	has, have, had given
go	went	has, have, had gone
grow	grew	has, have, had grown
know	knew	has, have, had known
lay	laid	has, have, had laid

Irregular Verbs *(continued)*

PRESENT TENSE	PAST TENSE	PAST PARTICIPLE
lie	lay	has, have, had lain
lose	lost	has, have, had lost
make	made	has, have, had made
ride	rode	has, have, had ridden
ring	rang	has, have, had rung
rise	rose	has, have, had risen
run	ran	has, have, had run
say	said	has, have, had said
see	saw	has, have, had seen
seek	sought	has, have, had sought
set	set	has, have, had set
shake	shook	has, have, had shaken
shine	shone	has, have, had shone
shrink	shrank	has, have, had shrunk
sing	sang	has, have, had sung
sink	sank	has, have, had sunk
sit	sat	has, have, had sat
slay	slew	has, have, had slain
speak	spoke	has, have, had spoken
spin	spun	has, have, had spun
spring	sprung	has, have, had sprung
steal	stole	has, have, had stolen
stick	stuck	has, have, had stuck
sting	stung	has, have, had stung
strive	strove	has, have, had striven
swear	swore	has, have, had sworn
swim	swam	has, have, had swum
swing	swung	has, have, had swung
take	took	has, have, had taken
teach	taught	has, have, had taught
tear	tore	has, have, had torn
throw	threw	has, have, had thrown
wear	wore	has, have, had worn
write	wrote	has, have, had written

And the Correct Verb Is . . .

DIRECTIONS: Complete each sentence by writing the correct form of the verb in parentheses in the blank.

1. The puppy _____ cautiously up to the old cat. **(creep)**

2. Mr. Liu has _____ science for 25 years in the same classroom. **(teach)**

3. Having never _____ before, Samantha was nervous as she waited for the plane to take off. **(fly)**

4. Tim was convinced he had _____ a UFO when he was camping last summer. **(see)**

5. In the story, the prince _____ the dragon and saved the princess. **(slay)**

6. Last year Jess _____ several laps each morning as part of her conditioning program. **(swim)**

7. Erin and her dad _____ a dozen fish on their previous fishing trip. **(catch)**

8. Todd was satisfied with the essay he had _____. **(write)**

9. Kelly and Tanya have _____ each other since third grade. **(know)**

10. Because of the cold weather, the pond has _____ early this winter. **(freeze)**

11. The rays of the early morning sun _____ into the room and brightened everyone's outlook. **(burst)**

12. Finding information for the report had _____ a serious problem for Cal. **(become)**

Verb Tenses

TEACHING SUGGESTIONS

The tense of a verb helps to show when something happened in a sentence. A common mistake of student writers is to shift tenses, causing confusion for the reader.

Activity 1 – Worksheet 51, "About Time . . ."

OBJECTIVE: Students are to identify the tenses of verbs in a set of sentences.

PROCEDURE: Distribute copies of List 51 and review the examples of verb tenses with your students. Explain that the tense of a verb indicates time in a sentence. Past tense shows action that has happened, present tense shows action that is happening now, and future tense shows action that will (or might) happen at a later date. Note that each of these tenses also has a "perfect" form that enables writers to be quite specific in their time setting of action.

Hand out copies of Worksheet 51. For the activity, students are to identify the tense of the verbs in the sentences.

ANSWER KEY: 1. past 2. present 3. past perfect 4. present 5. future perfect 6. present perfect 7. future 8. past perfect 9. past 10. future perfect 11. future 12. present perfect

Activity 2 – A Wish

OBJECTIVE: Students are to write an account of a special wish.

PROCEDURE: Hand out copies of List 51 and review the examples of verb tenses with your students. Explain that writers use the tense of verbs to indicate action that happened in the past, is happening, or will happen.

For the activity, students are to think of a wish. It might be a huge wish, for example, world peace, or something simple, perhaps wishing for snow and a day off from school tomorrow. Instruct your students to write an account of their wish. Suggest that, along with a description, they explain why this is their wish and what will happen if their wish were to come true. Encourage your students to focus on the correct use of verb tenses in their writing.

See List 50, "Irregular Verbs."

Verb Tenses

Verb tense helps to show when action or an event happens in a sentence. The main tenses are simple past, simple present, and simple future. A verb may also be one of three "perfect" tenses. These tenses require the use of *has, have,* or *had* with the past participle.

- *Past tense* shows action that has already happened. *Example:*

  Shannon spoke with Meg last week.

- *Present tense* shows action that is currently happening. *Example:*

  Shannon speaks with Meg every day.

- *Future tense* shows action that will (or might) happen. *Example:*

  Shannon will speak with Meg tomorrow.

- *Past perfect tense* shows a past action that ended before another past action started. It requires *had* with the past participle. *Example:*

  Shannon had spoken with Meg before eating dinner.

- *Present perfect tense* shows an action that started in the past and may continue in the present. It requires *has* or *have* with the past participle. *Example:*

  Shannon has spoken with Meg about the problem.

- *Future perfect tense* shows a future action that will have ended before another action begins. It requires *shall have* or *will have* with the past participle. *Example:*

  Shannon will have spoken with Meg before school.

About Time . . .

DIRECTIONS: Write the tense of each verb (or verb phrase) on the line after each sentence.

1. The softball game was postponed because of the heavy rain.

   _____

2. Tia receives phone calls all evening long from friends. _____

3. Cassandra had finished reading the novel two weeks before the rest of the class.

   _____

4. Mr. Harmon walks three miles before work each morning. _____

5. In just two more years, Ryan's older brother will have finished college.

   _____

6. Nicole has helped in her father's store every Saturday for years.

   _____

7. Melissa will go to Florida this summer to visit her aunt. _____

8. Tara's Uncle Sean had arrived from Ireland just in time for her birthday last year.

   _____

9. The valley received more than five feet of snow last winter. _____

10. By the end of next month, the committee will have submitted its recommendations.

    _____

11. Jan will be a doctor upon graduation. _____

12. Preston's group has started the first stage of its research. _____

52

Major Categories of Pronouns

TEACHING SUGGESTIONS

When students use pronouns incorrectly, it is often because they don't understand that different kinds of pronouns serve specific functions in a sentence. Adding to the confusion is informal speech in which people often use pronouns incorrectly. We have all heard—and probably used—constructions such as "Jim and me went to the game last night." Such common usage makes it hard for students to recall that the correct construction would be "Jim and I." Understanding the various categories of pronouns can help students use these words correctly.

Activity 1 – Worksheet 52, "Pick Your Pronouns"

OBJECTIVE: Students are to complete sentences by identifying the correct pronoun.

PROCEDURE: Distribute copies of List 52 and review the categories of pronouns with your students. Explain that, depending on its case, a pronoun serves a specific function in a sentence. For example, *nominative* case pronouns can only be used as subjects or predicate pronouns in a sentence, and *objective* case pronouns can only be used as objects. Emphasize that understanding the categories of pronouns can help students to use them correctly.

Hand out copies of Worksheet 52. For this activity, students are to complete each sentence by selecting the correct pronoun. Caution students to carefully consider the case of each pronoun before making their selections.

ANSWER KEY: 1. me   2. she   3. him   4. they   5. Whose   6. she   7. Their   8. Whom   9. Who   10. Your   11. us   12. She

Activity 2 – "A Family Tradition"

OBJECTIVE: Students are to write a description of a family tradition.

PROCEDURE: Hand out copies of List 52 and review the categories of pronouns with your students. Emphasize the importance of understanding these categories, for this will help students to use pronouns correctly.

For the activity, students are to write a description of a family tradition. Most families enjoy special events together; for example, an annual family reunion, a family picnic on the 4th of July, a summer vacation in the mountains, or a special celebration of a holiday. Instruct your students to write about their traditions. Remind them to use pronouns correctly in their writing.

See List 45, "Parts of Speech."

Major Categories of Pronouns

A pronoun is a word that takes the place of a noun. Pronouns have different forms, called *cases,* that indicate their purpose in a sentence. The major cases of pronouns follow.

NOMINATIVE CASE PRONOUNS

Nominative case pronouns take the place of nouns that are the subjects of a sentence. They may also take the place of nouns that follow a linking verb, in which instance they are known as predicate pronouns.

	Singular	*Plural*
First Person:	I	we
Second Person:	you	you
Third Person:	he, she, it	they

OBJECTIVE CASE PRONOUNS

Objective case pronouns take the place of nouns that are direct or indirect objects in a sentence. They may also take the place of nouns that are the object of prepositions.

	Singular	*Plural*
First Person:	me	us
Second Person:	you	you
Third Person:	him, her, it	them

POSSESSIVE PRONOUNS

Possessive pronouns show ownership. While some are used alone, others are used before nouns.

POSSESSIVE PRONOUNS USED ALONE

	Singular	*Plural*
First Person:	mine	ours
Second Person:	yours	yours
Third Person:	his, her, its	theirs

POSSESSIVE PRONOUNS USED BEFORE NOUNS

	Singular	*Plural*
First Person:	my	our
Second Person:	your	your
Third Person:	his, her, its	their

Note: Do not confuse possessive pronouns with contractions:

Possessive Pronoun	*Contraction*
your	you're (you are)
its	it's (it is)
their	they're (they are)

INDEFINITE PRONOUNS

Indefinite pronouns refer to a person, place, thing, or idea without identifying which specific one. Indefinite pronouns may be singular or plural; some may be both.

Singular		*Plural*	*Singular or Plural*
another	no one	both	all
anybody	nothing	few	any
each	one	many	more
either	other	others	most
everyone	somebody	several	none
everything	someone		some
much	something		
neither			

WHO, WHOM, AND WHOSE

Who and *whom* are used as interrogative pronouns, which ask a question. They are also used as relative pronouns, which introduce a subordinate clause. *Whose* is a possessive pronoun that shows ownership.

- *Who* is a nominative case pronoun. Use *who* whenever *he* or *she* can be substituted for it. *Examples:*

  Who ate the cake?

  He (she) ate the cake.

  Marsha Wilson, who is the first-place finisher, wins the $500 savings bond.
  . . . she is the first-place finisher.

- *Whom* is an objective case pronoun. Use *whom* whenever you can change the sentence from a question to a statement and substitute *him* or *her. Examples:*

  Whom did you e-mail?

  You e-mailed him (her).

  With whom are you speaking?

  You are speaking with him (her).

- *Whose* is a possessive pronoun. Do not confuse it with *who's,* which is a contraction for *who is. Examples:*

  Whose books are on the table?

  Who's at the door? (Who is at the door?)

Pick Your Pronouns

DIRECTIONS: Complete each sentence by writing the correct pronoun from the pair of pronouns in parentheses.

1. The package was addressed to _____. **(I, me)**

2. Dara, Teri, and _____ plan to go to the movies on Friday night. **(she, her)**

3. The athletic award was presented to Ann and _____. **(he, him)**

4. Miguel and _____ are working on the science project together. **(they, them)**

5. _____ books are on the counter? **(Who's, Whose)**

6. The first person to suspect the error was _____. **(she, her)**

7. _____ house is at the end of the block. **(There, Their)**

8. _____ did you speak with when you called the company? **(Who, Whom)**

9. _____ will be the leader of Group One? **(Who, Whom)**

10. "_____ keys are on the table," Jess told her brother. **(Your, You're)**

11. Uncle Joe sent _____ a gift from California. **(we, us)**

12. _____ and Charlene are best friends. **(She, Her)**

Common Prepositions

TEACHING SUGGESTIONS

Prepositions are words that relate a noun or pronoun to another word in a sentence. They enable writers to expand their sentences with details and images.

Activity 1 – Worksheet 53, "Preposition Hunt"

OBJECTIVE: Students are to identify the prepositions in an article.

PROCEDURE: Distribute copies of List 53 and review the prepositions with your students. Note that a preposition begins a prepositional phrase; a noun or pronoun serves as the preposition's object. Any words that describe the object of a preposition are also a part of the phrase. Emphasize that prepositional phrases can add details to sentences.

Hand out copies of Worksheet 53. Instruct your students to read the article and circle all of the prepositions.

EXTENSION: After they have circled all of the prepositions, instruct students to underline all of the prepositional phrases once and underline the object of each preposition twice.

ANSWER KEY: (In order, prepositions in phrases are italicized and objects of the prepositions are underlined):

in colder <u>climates</u>, *of* <u>temperature</u>, *around* the <u>world</u>, *over* the past <u>century</u>, *of* our <u>planet</u>, *of* the <u>1990s</u>, *on* <u>record</u>, *by* the <u>end</u>, *of* this <u>century</u>, *on* a planetary <u>scale</u>, *in* the <u>U.S.</u>, *of* <u>Louisiana</u> and <u>Florida</u>, *of* rising <u>temperatures</u>, *in* <u>climate</u>

Activity 2 – "An Ideal Job"

OBJECTIVES: Students are to write an article describing what would be their ideal summer or part-time job. Upon completion, they are to exchange their writing with a partner, proofread each other's work, and circle all prepositions.

PROCEDURE: Hand out copies of List 53 and review the prepositions with your students. Discuss the examples of prepositional phrases at the end of the list, noting that a noun or pronoun must be the object of a preposition.

For the activity, instruct your students to write about an ideal summer or part-time job. Encourage them to explain why this job would be ideal. Does the job pay well? Does it offer good hours? Does it offer the chance to do something meaningful or enjoyable? Upon completion, students are to exchange their writing with a partner, proofread each other's work, then identify the prepositions.

See List 45, "Parts of Speech."

Common Prepositions

A preposition is a word that relates a noun or a pronoun to another word in a sentence. The noun or pronoun that follows a preposition is called the *object* of the preposition. Together with any words that modify the object, the group of words is called a *prepositional phrase*. Prepositional phrases enable writers to add details to sentences. Following is a list of common prepositions and examples of prepositional phrases.

aboard	behind	in	till
about	below	inside	to
above	beneath	into	toward
across	beside	near	under
after	besides	of	underneath
against	between	off	until
along	beyond	on	unto
alongside	by	onto	up
among	down	out	upon
around	during	over	with
at	for	through	within
before	from	throughout	without

EXAMPLES OF PREPOSITIONAL PHRASES:

- He walked *into the room.*
- *Before school* Jason jogs *around the track.*
- Marissa paints *in a studio* that is *above her apartment.*
- The cave descended thirty feet *below the surface.*
- *During the storm,* the puppy hid *under the couch.*

Preposition Hunt

DIRECTIONS: Read the article and circle all of the prepositions.

The Earth's glaciers and polar icecaps are melting. Moreover, winters are getting shorter, and lakes and rivers in colder climates are freezing later and thawing earlier.

Measurements of temperature around the world indicate that the Earth is becoming hotter. Many scientists believe the cause is global warming. Over the past century, the average temperature of our planet has increased more than one degree Fahrenheit, and the decade of the 1990s was the warmest on record. Some scientists predict that by the end of this century, the Earth's average temperature may rise another five degrees.

That is a significant increase when measured on a planetary scale. As glaciers and polar ice continue melting, sea levels will rise. Coastal cities and towns will be flooded. In the United States, parts of Louisiana and Florida will be underwater. Climate will change, too. Even as bigger and more violent storms strike some areas, drought will parch others.

If the trend of rising temperatures is not stopped, the Earth will experience major changes in climate. People everywhere will be affected.

Prewriting Checklist

TEACHING SUGGESTIONS

The writing process consists of several stages. The first stage is prewriting, which includes topic selection, a purpose for writing, audience selection, method of delivery, idea generation, the focusing of ideas, research, analysis of information, and organization. It also includes free writing, which may lead into the writing of the first draft.

Not all writers adhere to each part of the prewriting stage as detailed here; nor do all follow the same prewriting pattern. For all, however, prewriting is essential, because it enables the writer to focus his or her attention on the development and organization of ideas for writing a particular piece.

Because of its importance to the overall writing process, you may wish to introduce List 54 relatively early in the school year. You may also wish to distribute copies of Background Sheet 54, "Simple Outline Format," that accompanies this list. The outline can help your students in organizing their material.

Activity 1 – Worksheet 54, "It's Your Pick"

OBJECTIVE: Students are to select a topic that has personal meaning and write an article.

PROCEDURE: Distribute copies of List 54, review the prewriting steps, and emphasize the importance of prewriting to your students. Explain that prewriting is the part of the overall writing process that prepares a writer for writing.

Hand out copies of Worksheet 54. For this activity, encourage your students to choose their own topics. For those who have trouble selecting a topic, suggest the following:

- How to Ask a Boy (or Girl) for a Date
- How to Keep Your Birthday Party Under Control
- The Best Advice You Can Offer Your Friends
- Tips for Managing School, Work, and Fun

Note that completing the worksheet, which guides students through prewriting, will help them develop their topic.

Activity 2 – Writing About Changes

OBJECTIVE: Students are to write an article about change and how it affects their lives.

PROCEDURE: Distribute copies of List 54. Discuss the writing process in general—there are several stages including prewriting, drafting, revising, editing, and publishing—and focus particular attention on prewriting. Discuss the importance of prewriting, then instruct your students to write an article about how change affects their lives. Encourage them to develop their own topics; however, you might offer these as examples:

- How Changing Schools Changed My Life
- How Getting Older Is Changing My Life
- How My Parents Influence Me

Instruct your students to develop their topics in accordance with the steps outlined in List 54. You might mention that for some topics they may not need to use all the steps.

See List 55, "Target Audience Checklist," and List 72, "The Writing Process."

Prewriting Checklist

Writing is a process composed of several stages. These stages can be broken down into prewriting, drafting, revising, editing, and publishing. Prewriting is the first stage of the process. Just as a builder needs plans and materials to construct a house, a writer needs to gather and organize information before he or she can expect to write clearly and effectively on a topic. Not all writers use all of the following prewriting activities; however, virtually all writers follow some type of prewriting plan. Prewriting enables a writer to generate and clarify his or her thoughts before beginning the actual writing.

SELECT A TOPIC:

List topics you are interested in writing about. Do background reading on possible topics. Choose a topic in which you are genuinely interested.

IDENTIFY A PURPOSE AND AN AUDIENCE:

Ask yourself what you want to write about on your topic. What is your intention? Do you want to entertain your readers, inform them, or persuade them to accept a particular point of view about an issue? You should also identify your target audience, the people for whom you are writing. This will help you focus your ideas.

CHOOSE A METHOD OF DELIVERY:

Once you have identified your purpose, decide on a method of delivery that will communicate your ideas effectively. Will you write an informational article, a story, a poem, a play, or an editorial? Knowing what kind of writing you will be doing can help guide you in the research and development of your material.

GENERATE AND BRAINSTORM IDEAS:

Write down all thoughts or ideas about your topic. Do not judge or attempt to organize the ideas at this point. The objective of brainstorming is to generate as many ideas about a topic as possible.

Prewriting Checklist *(continued)*

CONNECT IDEAS:

Read through your ideas and look for connections. How do the ideas relate to each other? Do any of the ideas give rise to other ideas?

FOCUS YOUR TOPIC:

After recognizing the broad scope of your topic, focus it so that it is specific. A broad topic is dogs; a focused topic is poodles. An even more focused topic is the history of poodles.

RESEARCH:

If necessary, conduct research to find more information. Information can be found in books, magazines, newspapers, tapes, films, and on the Internet. Interviews with people who can provide valuable insight, as well as first-hand observation, are also useful research methods.

ANALYZE INFORMATION:

As you develop ideas, ask yourself the questions: *who, what, when, where, why,* and *how*. Answering these questions can help you identify the most important details about a topic.

ORGANIZE INFORMATION:

Information must be organized so that it can be presented clearly and logically. Most nonfiction writing should have an opening, a body, and a conclusion. Your method of organization might be a simple list of main ideas and details, or it may be a comprehensive outline.

USE FREE WRITING:

Free writing is a method to jump-start your writing. Write about your topic without worrying about punctuation or grammar, or even about the flow of ideas. Ideas will come, and they will often surprise you!

It's Your Pick

DIRECTIONS: Select a topic that you find meaningful and write an article about it. Completing the worksheet first will help you organize your ideas.

1. What is your topic? _____

   _____

2. What is your purpose for writing this article? _____

   _____

   _____

   _____

3. List major ideas about your topic. _____

   _____

   _____

   _____

   _____

   _____

   _____

4. Will you need to research your topic? If yes, what sources will you consult?

   _____

   _____

   _____

   _____

   _____

5. On the back of this sheet, answer the questions *who, what, where, when, why,* and *how* about your topic.

6. Organize your information in list form or as a simple outline.

7. Write your first draft!

Background Sheet 54:

Simple Outline Format

Title _____

I. _____

    A. _____

    B. _____

    C. _____

II. _____

    A. _____

    B. _____

    C. _____

III. _____

    A. _____

    B. _____

    C. _____

Note: Add more main ideas and details as needed.

55

Target Audience Checklist

TEACHING SUGGESTIONS

Authors write to communicate ideas. The people to whom they direct those ideas are their audience. When writers know their audience, they can express ideas in a way that is likely to make the most sense to their readers. For instance, you would not explain lightning to a first grader in the same way that you would to a high school senior. When students identify their target audiences, their writing frequently assumes greater focus because they are directing their words to someone specific.

Activity 1 – Worksheet 55, "A Personal Message"

OBJECTIVES: Students are to write an editorial on a topic of their choice; they are to identify the target audience for their topic.

PROCEDURE: Distribute copies of List 55 and review the guidelines with your students. Discuss the importance of identifying a target audience for writing.

For the assignment, hand out copies of Worksheet 55. Instruct your students to select a problem or issue that is meaningful to them. The topic may be of local, national, or international interest. They are to write an editorial that expresses their views and tries to persuade others to accept their position. For students who have trouble finding a topic, you might suggest the following:

- The Use of Animals in Medical Research
- The Food in the School Cafeteria
- How a Person Can Make a Difference

Note that completing the worksheet first will help students organize their ideas.

Activity 2 – Persuading Your Peers

OBJECTIVE: Students are to write an article, trying to convince their classmates to support a special event.

PROCEDURE: Hand out copies of List 55 and review the guidelines with your students. For this assignment, ask your students to imagine that they are in charge of a special class event. This event can be real or imaginary; for example, a class dance, a fund-raiser, a play, or perhaps a class trip to Tahiti. Students are to write an article in which they describe the event and persuade their classmates to support it. Encourage students to follow the guidelines presented in the "Target Audience Checklist."

See List 54, "Prewriting Checklist."

Target Audience Checklist

Readers are a writer's audience. Because readers cannot ask questions of a writer as they read his or her material, the writing must be as clear as possible. When writers understand who their readers will be, they are better able to write in a manner that will make most sense to their audience. The following questions can help you focus your writing for specific readers.

1. Who will my readers be?

2. What is the general age of my readers?

3. What interests do my readers have?

4. What information do I want to share with them?

5. What would my readers like to learn from my writing?

6. Are my readers likely to find my material interesting? If yes, why? If no, why not?

7. Am I presenting my information in the right manner for my readers? How might I present it in a better way?

8. Do my readers already know this information? If yes, how can I offer it in a new, fresh, or insightful way?

9. What would be an interesting opening for my writing, one that will grab the attention of my audience?

10. What details and examples can I use that will make my writing interesting for my readers?

11. What would be a strong closing for my material?

12. If I were a member of my target audience, how would I react to my writing?

A Personal Message

DIRECTIONS: Pick a problem or issue that you find meaningful. You are to write an editorial that expresses your views and persuades others to accept your position. To help focus your editorial for your target audience, answer the questions below.

1. Who will my readers be? _____

   _____

2. What interests do my readers have? _____

   _____

   _____

   _____

3. Why is this material important to them? _____

   _____

   _____

   _____

4. What would be an interesting opening to my editorial? _____

   _____

   _____

   _____

5. What details and examples can I use to make my writing interesting to my readers?

   _____

   _____

   _____

6. What would be a strong closing for my editorial? _____

   _____

   _____

   _____

Checklist for Organizing Nonfiction

TEACHING SUGGESTIONS

Nonfiction is a major category of writing. It is likely that your students will write far more nonfiction than fiction. List 56 will be helpful to them in the writing of articles, essays, research papers, and book reports, as well as answering questions on essay tests. Utilizing this list regularly will help students become more proficient in developing their nonfiction writing.

Activity 1 – Worksheet 56, "A Person Who Made a Difference in My Life"

OBJECTIVE: Students are to write a personal account of a person who has significantly influenced them.

PROCEDURE: Distribute copies of List 56 and discuss the main parts of a nonfiction composition. Explain that virtually all nonfiction—articles, editorials, reports, essays, reviews—follows this basic pattern.

Explain that as our lives progress we realize that some people have greatly influenced us. Some of these people we know personally—a mother, a father, a friend, or a relative—while others we know only through what we've read or heard about them. These people include authors, historical figures, religious leaders, social leaders, and politicians. Ask your students to think of someone who has influenced them greatly. How have these people influenced them?

Hand out copies of Worksheet 56. Instruct your students to write an account of a person who has made a difference in their lives. Encourage them to complete the worksheet, which will help them to organize their ideas.

Activity 2 – Reviewing in Groups

OBJECTIVE: Working in small groups, students are to review magazine articles and identify the major parts of at least three articles.

PROCEDURE: A few days before beginning this activity, you might ask students to bring in magazines from home, or you might ask your school librarian if you can use some magazines from the school's library. You should have several magazines available for each group.

Distribute copies of List 56. Discuss the main parts of articles, then divide your students into groups of three or four. Instruct them to review the magazines and choose at least three articles. They are to discuss the articles and identify the opening, body, and conclusion of each.

See List 57, "Checklist for Revision," and List 59, "Proofreading Checklist."

Checklist for Organizing Nonfiction

The typical work of nonfiction has three parts: the opening, the body, and the conclusion. Keeping these parts in mind as you organize your information can help make the overall writing process easier.

THE OPENING (ALSO CALLED THE LEAD)

- Introduces the subject.

- Captures the reader's interest through the use of a *hook*. A hook may be a startling statement, an interesting fact, a question, a quotation, or an anecdote.

- Leads smoothly into the body.

THE BODY

- Develops the main ideas with specific details, facts, and examples.

- Answers the questions *who, what, when, where, why,* and *how* for the main ideas.

THE CONCLUSION (ALSO CALLED THE CLOSING)

- May contain a final idea, a call for action, or a brief summary of the main idea.

A Person Who Made a Difference in My Life

DIRECTIONS: Think of a person who has made a major difference in your life. This individual might be a parent, sibling, relative, friend, teacher, cleric, political leader, or historical figure. Use the simple outline form below to help you organize your thoughts; then write an article about this person and how he or she has influenced you.

Opening: _____

_____

_____

_____

_____

Body: _____

_____

_____

_____

_____

_____

_____

_____

_____

_____

_____

_____

Conclusion: _____

_____

_____

_____

_____

Checklist for Revision

TEACHING SUGGESTIONS

Revision is a vital part of the writing process. It is the stage when ideas take their final shape, style is polished, and mechanics are checked. Revision (which means "to see again") centers around rewriting. A few words or phrases may be changed, or paragraphs or entire pages may be rewritten. Revision might lead to a new opening, a new closing, substantial cuts or additions, elaboration, a change in viewpoint or structure, a change in sequence, or a new focus. The type and amount of revision varies with each piece. Unfortunately, revision is also one of the more difficult parts of writing to teach. Many students consider their writing finished as soon as they place the final period on their papers.

You can reduce much of your students' resistance to revision by treating it as an expected part of every assignment. Revision should come after each draft has been completed. While some revision, of course, will go on as the draft is being written—ideas may change a bit, phrases may be reworked, some experimentation with words may go on—encourage your students to avoid excessive revision during the draft, for this may interfere with creativity. It is during the draft stage that a writer's emotions are often at their keenest level, and excessive revision at this time may undermine the flow of ideas.

Activity 1 – Worksheet 57, "It's Tough Being Young," and Worksheet 57a, "Revision Rating Sheet"

OBJECTIVE: Students are to read an essay and score it according to a revision rating sheet.

PROCEDURE: Distribute copies of List 57 and review the items on the checklist with your students. Explain the importance of revision, and emphasize that no piece of writing is done until it has been revised.

Hand out copies of Worksheets 57 and 57a. Explain that students are to read the essay (57) and score it according to the rating sheet (57a). The scoring is simple. Students answer the questions on the rating sheet either yes or no. If they answer no, they are to include a reason on the back of the sheet. You might mention that the essay has several weaknesses. After your students have rated the essay, they are to tally the score. Point values are explained on the rating sheet.

Now for the fun. Take a poll and ask how many students rated the essay between 1 and 5, 6 and 10, and 11 and 15. (A perfect score is 15.) It is likely that you will get a variety of scores. Discuss the results and ask students to justify their scoring. You might also wish to have students offer some ways to revise the essay.

While students will undoubtedly rate the essay differently, some weaknesses stand out:

- The author doesn't stick to the purpose.
- The opening is weak because no details are offered.
- The author rambles with the development; he or she seems to be writing two different essays.
- Too many short, choppy, incomplete sentences make the essay rough.
- Ideas are not fully developed.
- There is little logical development.
- The conclusion is weak.

(*Note:* You can use the rating sheet with other pieces of writing.)

Activity 2 – Revising the Essay

OBJECTIVE: Students are to rewrite an essay that has several weaknesses.

PROCEDURE: You may have the class do this assignment in conjunction with Activity 1 or separately. Begin by handing out copies of List 57 and reviewing the checklist with your students. Note the importance of revision to proficient writing.

Distribute copies of Worksheet 57 and explain that students are to revise the essay. Point out that the essay has several weaknesses, and note that during revision students may need to add or delete material, smooth sentence structure, or change the focus. At the end of the activity, discuss the revised essays and have students read excerpts of their revisions so that they can see the different ways a piece can be revised.

See List 58, "Checklist for Revising Fiction."

Checklist for Revision

Revision is an important part of writing. It is the time a writer revisits his or her work for the purpose of making it better. Writing is not finished until it has been revised. Use the following questions as a guide for revision.

1. Have I written what I started out to write?

2. Have I identified my audience and written for them?

3. Does my opening capture the attention of my readers?

4. Does my opening lead smoothly into the body?

5. Have I developed my ideas logically in the body of my writing?

6. Have I written an effective conclusion?

7. Have I stayed on my topic, or have I strayed and included unnecessary information?

8. Have I presented my ideas clearly to my readers?

9. Have I supported my main ideas with specific details and examples?

10. Are my facts accurate?

11. Does each sentence communicate exactly what I want to say?

12. Have I used complete sentences?

13. Have I begun my sentences with capital letters?

14. Have I used correct punctuation?

15. Have I indented paragraphs?

16. Does each paragraph have only one main idea?

17. Have I used transitions between paragraphs?

18. Have I used correct spelling?

19. Have I used each word correctly?

20. What do I like best about this piece?

It's Tough Being Young

DIRECTIONS: Read the following essay carefully and rate it according to your Revision Rating Sheet. Be prepared to support your scoring.

It's tough being young. There are a lot of reasons I feel like that.

I wish I was older. Not old. Older. Say about 25. Then I'd be on my own and I'd be able to do what I want.

I wouldn't have to listen to my parents anymore. I mean I'd be willing to talk to them, but I wouldn't have to do what they told me to. I could make my own decisions.

I wouldn't have to do homework either. I'd be done with school. Forever.

I'd probably have a job—I think I'd like to own my own business. What kind of business? I'm not sure about that. But I'd like to own one. It'd be great being the boss. Giving orders and things.

I'd have a car, too, if I was older. And I'd be able to go wherever I wanted.

That's why it's tough being young.

Revision Rating Sheet

DIRECTIONS: Use this sheet to rate nonfiction writing. Read the piece and answer the following questions "yes" or "no." Give a reason for your "no" answers on the back of the sheet. When you are finished, tally the score. For questions 1 through 10, each "yes" answer counts for 1 point, and "no" answers receive 0 points. The answer for question 11 is added to the overall score. (For example, if you gave the piece a 3 for question 11, you would add 3 to the total number of "yes" answers.) A perfect score is 15.

Title: _____

	YES	NO
1. Did the author write according to his/her purpose?	____	____
2. Did the author write for a specific audience?	____	____
3. Did the opening capture attention?	____	____
4. Were the author's ideas developed logically?	____	____
5. Did the author stay on the topic?	____	____
6. Were the ideas presented clearly?	____	____
7. Were the main ideas supported with details?	____	____
8. Were correct mechanics used?	____	____
9. Was correct spelling used?	____	____
10. Was the conclusion strong?	____	____

11. On the basis of 1 to 5, with 5 being the highest, I'd rate this piece a . . . ____

Total Score: ____

THE WRITING TEACHER'S BOOK OF LISTS

Checklist for Revising Fiction

TEACHING SUGGESTIONS

Editors and teachers of writing all too often come across student stories that in a purely mechanical sense are fine, yet lack important elements. For some reason a story may not be fully convincing, the characters may not seem entirely believable, or the story is of the ho-hum, so-what variety—in other words, it lacks conflict and action. The story has no impact.

While a reader, particularly a trained one such as an editor or a teacher, can generally spot the weaknesses in a story easily, the task of zeroing in on weaknesses can be difficult for the writer. He or she may be too close to the story and too emotionally involved with it to see it objectively. An honest rundown of the questions presented in the accompanying list can be most useful to these writers, for it can help them identify the weaknesses in their stories, which is the first step of effective revision.

Activity 1 – Worksheet 58, "The Guest"

OBJECTIVE: Students are to revise a story.

PROCEDURE: Distribute copies of List 58 and discuss the questions for revision with your students. Emphasize the importance of revision to writing and remind students that revision can include adding and deleting material, writing new openings, enhancing development, improving climaxes, and correcting mechanics.

Next, hand out copies of Worksheet 58. Explain that students are to revise the story and point out that the story contains various mistakes and weaknesses. They should revise their stories on a separate sheet of paper.

ANSWER KEY: Revised stories may vary; following is one possibility.

"It's not fair!" Danielle said. "Just when I finally get my own room I have to give it up again."

"I'm sorry, Danielle," her mother said, "but there's no choice. Your grandfather has to live with us until he recovers from his operation."

Although she knew that her mother was right, Danielle was still angry. For the past few years she had waited for her older brother to go to college so that she could have his bedroom. She didn't want to share a bedroom with her younger sister again.

"You don't understand," Danielle said.

"I understand well enough to know that things don't always work out the way we want," her mother said. "This is going to be harder on Pop than it is on us. He's always been a very independent man."

Danielle was about to say more, but through the living room window she saw the ambulance pull into the driveway. She watched the attendants help her grandfather into the wheelchair. She was surprised at how he had changed. This wasn't the rugged man she had always known.

She felt sorry for him and knew that her mother was right. She hurried to the door.

"Hi, Grandpop," she said. "It's going to be nice having you with us."

Activity 2 – Self-Editing

OBJECTIVE: Students are to reread and revise a story they had previously written.

PROCEDURE: Hand out copies of List 58 and discuss the questions regarding revision with your students. For this activity, instruct your students to review a story they have already written. Referring to the questions on List 58, they are to revise any parts of their stories they now feel would benefit from reworking. A new final copy should be produced. At the end of the activity, you might ask volunteers to share what they felt was necessary to revise in their papers, as well as how they went about the revision.

See List 57, "Checklist for Revision."

Checklist for Revising Fiction

The following questions can be helpful in revising fiction.

1. Is my story believable? Does it make sense?

2. Are my characters realistic? Do they act like real people within the setting of the story?

3. Do my characters talk like real people?

4. Do my characters dress like people would during the time my story takes place?

5. Do the actions of my characters arise from their personalities? Do they behave according to their natures?

6. Have I used quotation marks to indicate dialogue?

7. Does my story have conflict, or a problem that must be solved?

8. Are my scenes realistic? Do they paint pictures in the minds of my readers?

9. Is my story unified? Do all the parts build to a whole?

10. Does every scene move toward the climax?

11. Is my climax exciting? Is it a logical ending to the development of my story?

12. Does my conclusion tie together all the loose ends of my story?

13. Is there any material I can eliminate from my story?

14. If I had to change something about my story, what would I change?

15. Is my story satisfying?

The Guest

DIRECTIONS: Read the following story carefully. It has weaknesses in structure, punctuation, spelling, word usage, capitalization, and sentence construction. Rewrite the story, improving its weaknesses.

"It's not far!" Danielle said. Just when I finally get my own room I have to give it up again."

"I'm sorry, Danielle," her mother said, "But there's no choice. Your grandfather has to live with us until he recovers from his operation."

She knew that her mother was right, Danielle was still angry. For the past few years she had waited for her older brother to go to college so that she could have his bedroom. She thought of her brother in college now. She imagined that he was having a lot of fun. She didnt want to share a bedroom with her younger sister again.

"you don't understand." Danielle said.

"I understand well enough to know that things don't always work out the way we want," her mother said. "this is going to be harder on Pop than it is on us. He's always been a very independent man."

Danielle was about to say more, but threw the living room window she saw the ambulance pull into the driveway. She watched the attendants help her grandfather into the wheelchair. She was suprised at he had changed. This was'nt the rugged man she had always knew.

She felt sorry for him and knew that her mother is right. She hurried to the door.

"Hi, Grandpop," she said. "Its going to be nice having your with us."

Proofreading Checklist

TEACHING SUGGESTIONS

Proofreading requires concentration and an understanding of the mechanics of writing. After a piece has been written and revised, it must be proofread. The purpose of proofreading is to find any remaining errors, usually in mechanics, that might have been overlooked during revisions. Proofreading is difficult for many students, who may not understand the rules of grammar and punctuation.

When teaching proofreading, review the basic rules of mechanics with your students and encourage them to refer to their language texts or writer's style-books when they are unsure of a specific rule. Mention that authors often turn to such sources.

Activity 1 – Worksheet 59, "The New Kid in Town"

OBJECTIVE: Students are to proofread and correct a story.

PROCEDURE: Distribute copies of List 59 and review the items from the checklist with your students. Explain that proofreading is an essential part of the writing process, because it offers the writer a final chance to correct any mistakes that were previously overlooked.

Hand out copies of Worksheet 59. Explain that students are to proofread and correct the story; note that the story contains several errors in mechanics. Students are to find the errors and rewrite the story correctly.

ANSWER KEY: Jennifer stopped at the corner and looked at her new school. It was enormous. She wanted to turn around and run home.

Jennifer and her parents had moved to Rosemont the day before, and this was to be her first day in school. Jennifer was worried that the kids wouldn't like her and that she wouldn't be able to find her way around.

Gathering her courage—which wasn't easy—she walked the final block and reported to the office. She had registered there yesterday.

"Hello, Jennifer," said the secretary, remembering her. After checking some papers, she handed Jennifer a lock for her locker. "Your locker is number ninety-seven. It's down the hall to your right."

Jennifer thanked the woman and left. The halls were crowded, but Jennifer finally found her locker. As she opened it, she heard a friendly voice.

"Hi. My name's Lisa."

Jennifer turned. "Hi," she said, "I'm Jennifer Logan."

"Are you new here?" Lisa said with a bright smile.

Jennifer nodded.

"Well, you're going to like it here," Lisa said. "The school's not bad and the kids are super. What's your first class?"

When Jennifer showed Lisa her schedule, the other girl said, "We're in the same class. Come on. I'll show you the way."

Activity 2 – Proofreading Practice

OBJECTIVE: Students are to proofread a story of their own.

PROCEDURE: Hand out copies of List 59 and review the items with your students. Ask them to use the information on the list to proofread an article or story they have written. Encourage them to look for subtle mistakes in mechanics that might have slipped into their work and that they overlooked during revision.

See List 47, "Rules for Capitalization," List 48, "Rules for Punctuation," List 57, "Checklist for Revision," and List 58, "Checklist for Revising Fiction."

Proofreading Checklist

Your writing is *not* finished after revision. You must still edit and proofread your work. The purpose of proofreading is to find any remaining mistakes in mechanics that you might have overlooked while writing and revising. While the following list *does not include* every rule on mechanics, it provides the basic ones and makes a good guide for proofreading. If you are unsure of any rules, consult your language text or a writer's stylebook.

1. Is the ending punctuation correct?

   - Periods for declarative and imperative sentences

   - Question marks for interrogative sentences

   - Exclamation points for sentences that show strong emotion

2. Are periods used for abbreviations?

3. Are commas used correctly?

   - For lists

   - To separate phrases or clauses

   - For dates

   - Between city and state

   - After direct address

   - In dialogue

4. Are semicolons used to join independent clauses in a sentence?

5. Are colons used correctly?

   - To set off a list

   - For time

6. Are quotation marks used correctly?

   - "It is raining," John said.

   - "Is it raining?" John asked.

   - "Since it is raining," John said, "our baseball game will be canceled."

   - "It is raining," John said. "Our baseball game will be canceled."

   - For titles of stories, articles, songs, poems, and the chapters of books.

7. Are verb tenses correct? Is the use of tenses consistent (no unnecessary shifts between past, present, and future)?

8. Are proper nouns, proper adjectives, and the beginning of sentences capitalized?

9. Are paragraphs indented?

10. Is spelling correct throughout the piece?

11. Is underlining (italics) used for the titles of books, plays, and movies, and the names of newspapers and magazines?

12. Are apostrophes used correctly?

    - For possessive nouns

    - For contractions

The New Kid in Town

DIRECTIONS: Proofread the following story and find mistakes in mechanics. Rewrite the story, correcting the mistakes.

Jennifer stopped at the corner and looked at her new school. It was enormous she wanted to turn around and run home.

Jennifer and her parents had moved to Rosemont the day before and this was to be her first day of school Jennifer was worried that the kids wouldn't like her and that she wouldn't be able to find her way around.

Gathering her courage which wasn't easy Jennifer walked the final block and reported to the office. She had registered there yesterday.

"Hello Jennifer," said the secretary, remembering her. After checking some papers she handed Jennifer a lock for her locker. Your locker is number ninety-seven. Its down, the hall to your right."

Jennifer thanked the woman and left. The halls were crowded but Jennifer finally found her locker. As she opened it, she heard a friendly voice.

"Hi, my name's Lisa."

Jennifer turned. "Hi, she said "I'm Jennifer Logan."

"Are you new here?" Lisa said with a bright smile.

Jennifer nodded.

"Well you're going to like it here," Lisa said. "The school's not bad and the kids are super. What's your first class."

When Jennifer showed Lisa her schedule, the other girl said We're in the same class. Come on. I'll show you the way."

SPECIAL LISTS FOR
Student Writers

Traits of Good Writers

While every writer has his or her own ideas, style, and methods for writing, all good writers share many of the same traits. Good writers:

- Write every day, or as often as possible. Many writers keep journals in which they record their thoughts and impressions.

- Find and develop interesting ideas for writing.

- Try different forms of writing.

- Are curious and want to understand why things are as they are.

- Strive to communicate their ideas to others to enlighten, to entertain, or to persuade.

- Conduct research when necessary.

- Make sure all facts are accurate.

- Learn and apply the rules of written English.

- Revise and edit their material to make it the best it can be.

- Are persistent in completing their writing no matter how difficult.

- Enjoy reading as a part of their quest for knowledge, as well as for entertainment and a means to see how other writers construct their material.

- Have favorite authors, whose work they admire.

- Continue to grow as writers.

Story Parts

Stories can be broken down into several major parts. When writers understand these parts, they are more likely to create interesting stories.

- *Setting:* The setting is the location in which the events and action of a story take place. Depending on its length, a story might have several settings. A setting may be a school, a neighborhood, a city, the Old West, or a moon base. Realistic settings provide the background for interesting stories.

- *Characters:* The characters of a story are the people who take part in the story. Most stories have lead (main) and supporting characters. In science fiction and fantasy, characters may not be human and may be aliens, animals, demons, ogres, ghosts, or something entirely new arising from the author's imagination. Interesting, believable characters help to hold a reader's attention.

- *Plot:* The plot of a story consists of the events and actions that move the story forward. In the typical plot, the lead character, or characters, face a problem that they must solve. As the characters try to solve the problem, they run into complications that prevent them from solving the problem. Complications usually make the problem worse. By the end of the story, characters either solve or fail to solve the problem.

- *Conflict:* Conflict arises from the attempts of the characters to solve the problem. The lead characters may come into conflict with other characters, nature, the supernatural, themselves, or a combination of these elements. Conflict may be physical or emotional and usually results in the characters taking action.

- *Mood:* The mood of a story or scene is the feeling it causes in the reader. The mood may be suspenseful, frightening, lighthearted, or thrilling. It arises from a combination of factors, including the setting, action, and characters.

- *Climax:* The climax of a story is the event in which the lead characters either solve or fail to solve the problem.

- *Theme:* The theme of a story is the author's message or insight about the world that he or she reveals throughout the story. Common themes include: *Love conquers all* and *good triumphs over evil.*

Guidelines for Finding Ideas for Writing

Ideas for writing are everywhere! The following guidelines can help you discover countless ideas for stories, articles, and poems.

- *Personal Experience:* Things that happen to you — no matter how big or how little — can be seeds that grow and bloom into topics for writing. Think of the things that have occurred in your life and develop some into ideas for writing.

- *Special Interests:* Things that you find interesting can often prove to be interesting to others. A special talent or unusual hobby can result in an interesting story or article.

- *Observations:* Events you have seen or heard about, or questions that you have about the world, yourself, or others can be the springboard to writing ideas. Things that cause you wonder can turn out to be excellent topics.

- *Relationships:* Look for relationships and connections between things. When ideas connect to other ideas, they may lead you to interesting subjects that can be developed into fresh topics for writing. Global warming, for example, might result in drastic climate change, which in turn might lead to loss of habitats for animals, which in turn might cause these animals to become endangered. All of these ideas can be developed into stories and articles.

- *Viewing Ideas, Events, and Issues from Fresh Perspectives:* New ideas can often be found by looking at the ordinary in an unordinary way. Identify the way most people think about an issue and consider the opposite. Rather than thinking how a flood may affect people living in a town, imagine what it could do to the surrounding environment and wildlife.

- *What If's:* Take a situation or condition and ask what if. What if time stopped? What if the sun did not rise tomorrow? What if you woke up and you were a different person? What if . . . ?

100 Writing Cues

Even the most imaginative writers have days when they have trouble finding an idea to write about. The following list offers some suggestions.

Write about . . .

1. A time when everything was right and you felt on top of the world.

2. A time you did *not* complete a project or homework assignment, and explain why.

3. A person you respect.

4. Yourself, as if seeing yourself through the eyes of another.

5. An event or problem that really bothers you and how you would fix it.

6. Where you think you will be in five years and what you think you will be doing.

7. Your ideal room (assuming you can furnish and arrange it any way you wish).

8. One of your worst fears.

9. An imaginary meeting with a favorite character from one of your favorite books.

10. The happenings of today.

11. The advice for coping with life that you could give to a brother, sister, or friend.

12. Returning to school after a long break, in the form of a poem.

13. The best movie you have ever watched.

14. The worst movie you have ever watched.

15. Convincing a friend to read one of your favorite books.

16. The way you relax when you are stressed.

17. An outdoor scene, describing it with as much detail as possible.

18. A hobby or special talent you have.

19. What you believe are the traits of a successful person.

20. A question, problem, or event you found to be perplexing.

21. Why you feel you are the person who should be hired for your dream job.

22. Your town and what makes it different from other places to live.

23. Your idea for a new TV show.

24. An event in your past that has deeply influenced you.

25. Your family tree; your roots.

26. An event or incident in your life that you would change if you could.

27. An embarrassing moment.

28. What you consider to be a teenager's five most important rules of life.

29. Your greatest childhood fear.

30. A pet or favorite animal.

31. Your home and how you would remodel it.

32. Your goals for the next twelve months, or stretch things, for the next five years.

33. The perfect vacation (assuming money is no concern).

34. An imaginary interview with one of your favorite celebrities or sports stars.

35. The hero in a favorite story.

36. The villain in a favorite story.

37. An issue in your school that you feel strongly about.

38. An inanimate object that suddenly comes alive.

39. A place you would like to visit.

40. A person in history you would have liked to be.

41. The traits that make you a good friend to others.

42. A strange (imaginary) person who moves into your neighborhood.

43. Your pet—if your pet could talk, what would it say about you?

44. A description of a scene in nature, a busy street, a quiet park, or another place of your choice.

45. A description of your closet and the items inside.

46. An old photograph and the event it has recorded.

47. A poem describing your emotions and mood today, right now.

48. A list of ten good qualities that people should have.

49. An event in which you witnessed the power of nature.

50. A scene of your favorite character from a favorite movie, but in a different movie.

51. An imaginary creature.

52. A character sketch of your opposite.

53. A gift you would give someone you cared about.

54. Having the ability to do something nice for someone else.

55. What faith means to you.

56. An object, machine, or appliance in your life that you could not do without.

57. The ideal place for you to live.

58. A story that a parent, grandparent, uncle, or aunt told you.

59. Your favorite day of the week and why it is your favorite.

60. The solution to a recent problem.

61. Advice you would give to others about how to solve problems.

62. A poem about nature—perhaps a leaf, the blue sky, or a mountain.

63. A recent dream and its possible hidden meaning.

64. A folktale about writing.

65. An information packet about your school.

66. One thing the world needs more of.

67. Your exploits as the hero of a computer game.

68. A favorite place, using images created with all five senses.

69. A story about being caught in a natural catastrophe such as a flood, tornado, hurricane, or blizzard.

70. A story about you and a brother or sister (or another relative) suddenly and mysteriously trading places.

71. A story about your family, but instead of living in the 21st century, you are living in the past or future.

72. Advice you could give adults about raising children.

73. How your school could be improved.

74. Your strengths and weaknesses as a writer.

75. A scene from a favorite story from the point of view of a minor character.

76. Being a famous celebrity and your typical day.

77. Your favorite type of music, singer, or group.

78. How you changed in the last year.

79. An article detailing the types of excuses kids give to teachers as to why they haven't finished their homework.

80. A myth of modern times.

81. A scene of conflict—either character versus character, character versus nature, or character versus him- or herself.

82. A special event or holiday.

83. A time you first learned to do something.

84. How you would improve yourself.

85. A description of a symbol or logo that best symbolizes you.

86. An act of kindness that someone else once did for you (or you did for someone else).

87. An acceptance speech for an award you received.

88. A poem about life as you understand it.

89. An imaginary party given by your favorite singer—and you are invited!

90. A story in which you meet a visitor from another planet.

91. A historical event that fascinates you.

92. Living in the future. What would your life be like?

93. A special friend and what makes this person special.

94. A time you experienced true adventure.

95. About where (other than where you are now) you would like to be and why.

96. What your best friend would write about you in his or her diary.

97. Being in a museum when an ancient artifact begins to glow.

98. A greeting card to a friend or loved one.

99. A letter to a person in history.

100. Yourself and how you might improve as a writer.

Editor's Proofreading Marks

Use the following symbols when proofreading.

Mark ·	Meaning	Example
¶	new paragraph	. . . came home.¶Next . . .
∧	insert	
	- a letter	comittee
	- a word	They walked school.
	- a comma	sandwiches pie, and fruit
⊙	a period	They went home⊙
◠◯	move	They went ⟨later⟩ to the store
ℒ	delete	
	- a letter	The bedar growled.
	- a word	He did ~~did~~ his work.
∽	switch	
	- letters	The movie wsa great.
	- words	They went ⟨the⟩⟨to⟩ movie.
≡	capitalize	United states
/	small letter	The Actor smiled.
NC	not clear	NC Yesterday they are hiking.
│	separate	They went to school.
◡	combine	Put on your seat belt.
∨ ∨	quotation marks	Hello he said.

Types of Writing

Some writers fall into the habit of producing the same type of material when, in fact, there are many types of writing they can try.

advertisements

advice columns

allegories

anecdotes

autobiographies

awards

ballads

biographies

book reviews

cartoons

comic strips

diaries

editorials

essays

fables

fairy tales

fiction (adventure, contemporary, fantasy, historical, mystery, romance, science fiction)

folktales

greeting cards

how-to articles

informational articles

instructions

interviews

jokes

journals

letters (apology, business, complaint, congratulation, friendly, job application, to the editor)

movie reviews

myths

newsletters

newspaper articles

plays

poetry (nonrhyme, rhyme, concrete, cinquain, haiku, limerick, lyrical)

puzzles

quizzes

radio scripts

research papers

résumés

screenplays (for movies)

speeches

tall tales

TV and movie scripts

Common Writing Mistakes (and How to Fix Them)

All writers make mistakes. This is why revision and editing are so important to the writing process. Some mistakes and examples of weak writing are more common than others, and some of the most common are listed below.

1. Incorrect use of possessive nouns. *Examples:*

   Caryns' pencil (incorrect)   Caryn's pencil (correct)

   puppies's toys (incorrect)   puppies' toys (correct)

   childrens' bikes (incorrect)   children's bikes (correct)

2. Incorrect use of possessive pronouns and certain contractions. *Examples:*

   you're coat (incorrect)   your coat (correct)

   they're boat (incorrect)   their boat (correct)

   also there boat (incorrect)

   who's book (incorrect)   whose book (correct)

3. Incorrect use of *who* and *whom. Examples:*

   Whom is the leader of the group? (incorrect)

   Who is the leader of the group (correct)

   Who are you talking to? (incorrect)

   Whom are you talking to? (correct)

4. Incorrect subject/verb agreement. *Example:*

   Some students in the class believes there is too much homework. (incorrect)

   Some students in the class believe there is too much homework. (correct)

5. Incorrect use of irregular verbs. *Examples:*

   He seen the accident. (incorrect)

   He saw the accident. (correct)

   He had seen the accident. (correct)

6. Incorrect word usage, especially with homophones. *Example:*

   The plain took off on schedule. (incorrect)

   The plane took off on schedule. (correct)

7. Incorrect use of subject and object pronouns. *Examples:*

   Jess and me are going to the movies. (incorrect)

   Jess and I are going to the movies. (correct)

   The pizza was delivered to Theo and I. (incorrect)

   The pizza was delivered to Theo and me. (correct)

8. Incorrect use of pronouns and antecedents. *Example:*

   The student who lost their glasses should report to the office. (incorrect)

   The student who lost his (or her) glasses should report to the office. (correct)

9. The use of double negatives. *Examples:*

   Nobody had no ideas for research topics. (incorrect)

   Nobody had any ideas for research topics. (correct)

   Nobody had ideas for research topics. (correct)

10. Shifts in verb tense. *Example:*

    They went to the museum yesterday. They especially enjoy the exhibit on dinosaurs. (incorrect)

    They went to the museum yesterday. They especially enjoyed the exhibit on dinosaurs. (correct)

11. The use of run-ons. *Example:*

    Marcy came home from school, she started her homework, she went to dance practice. (run-on)

    Marcy came home from school, started her homework, and went to dance practice. (correct)

12. Incorrect use of quotation marks for dialogue. *Example:*

    It looks like snow, Jim said. (incorrect)

    "It looks like snow," Jim said. (correct)

Common Writing Mistakes (and How to Fix Them) *(continued)*

Although the next three are not in the strictest sense mistakes, they are examples of weak writing that should be avoided.

13. Use of general instead of specific descriptions. *Example:*

    The woman walked into the room. (okay)

    The gray-haired woman walked into the room. (better)

14. Use of passive instead of active voice. *Example:*

    I was given the package by Val. (passive)

    Val gave me the package. (active)

15. Use of weak verbs instead of strong verbs. *Example:*

    The little girl came softly into the room. (weak)

    The little girl tiptoed into the room. (stronger)

Guidelines for Writing a Query Letter

The purpose of a query letter is to interest an editor in your writing. The typical query describes your story or article in a manner that interests an editor enough so that he or she asks to see the manuscript. While there is no "standard" form for query letters, the following guidelines are helpful.

1. Limit your query letter to one page, single-spaced, double-spaced between paragraphs.

2. Use standard business letter format and address the letter to a specific editor. Make sure you have the editor's correct name and title. (Do not assume T. A. Jones is a mister. She might be Ms. Jones. If you are not certain, address the letter to T. A. Jones.)

3. Begin the letter with a strong opening that clearly contains your idea.

4. Briefly explain how you will develop the idea. Mention whether you will be including artwork or photographs with the manuscript. Also mention the approximate length of the manuscript.

5. Describe your background and why you are qualified to write about this topic. If you have had something published, mention it. (For example, writing for the school newspaper is valuable experience and worthwhile to mention.)

6. Ask the editor if he or she would like to see your material.

7. Thank the editor for his or her time and consideration.

8. Include an SASE (self-addressed, stamped envelope) for a reply. Many publications will not answer queries unless the writer includes an SASE.

Note: Many publications today accept e-mail queries. Whenever contacting editors through e-mail, use standard English. Remember, you are not chatting on-line with friends.

Manuscript Preparation

The appearance of your article or story is a reflection of your attitude about writing. A sloppy manuscript, one filled with grammatical and spelling mistakes, or wrinkled because it was shoved in a folder, shows that a writer does not value his or her own work. And if a writer places little value on his or her work, why should anyone else? Following are guidelines for preparing your story or article for editors.

1. Proofread carefully and try to make your final copy as error-free as possible.

2. Print your manuscript on clean 20-lb. white bond.

3. Place your name, address, phone number, and e-mail address at the upper left-hand corner of the title page or the first page of the manuscript. This information should be single-spaced.

4. Place the approximate word count in the upper right-hand corner.

5. For articles and stories, center the title about one-third down from the top of the first page. Write your name beneath the title. (For books, use a separate title page with the title centered about halfway from the top.)

6. Text should be double-spaced.

7. At least one-inch margins should be maintained on the top, bottom, and sides of every page.

8. Include a page heading at the top left of every page, starting with the second page. A typical page heading includes your name and a few key words of the title.

9. Pages should be numbered, preferably at the top right.

10. Except for the first page, the opening pages of chapters, and the last pages of chapters, every page should have the same number of lines.

11. Use a clear, easy-to-read font, such as Courier New, 12 point. Avoid fancy fonts. They will not impress editors and may cause eyestrain.

12. Use paper clips to hold the manuscript together. Do not staple the pages.

13. Mail stories, articles, and poems in a flat 9- by 12-inch envelope.

Manuscript Preparation *(continued)*

14. Always include an SASE (self-addressed, stamped envelope). Most editors will not return any materials unless you include an SASE.

15. Always keep copies of any material you send.

Note: While some publishers accept electronic submissions, many do not. Only send material via the Internet if you know the publisher accepts such submissions.

Markets for the Writing of Students

A number of magazines, both print and on-line, publish the writing of students. Encourage your students to submit material, but warn them that the competition is keen and that they should send only their best work. Since markets change frequently and some have special needs regarding submissions, you should contact each magazine, or check its Web site, for its guidelines. If possible, obtain copies of magazines (or view them on-line) to see what types of material they accept. Perhaps some of the print magazines are available in your school library. If not, maybe you can persuade your librarian to order them. Seeing the work of other young people can motivate your students to write their best.

PRINT MARKETS

Creative Kids
P.O. Box 8813
Waco, TX 76144–8813
www.prufrock.com/prufrock_jm_createkids.cfm
Stories, articles, editorials, poems, plays, and so on. Ages 8 to 14

Merlyn's Pen
P.O. Box 910
East Greenwich, RI 02818
www.merlynspen.com
Stories, poems, essays, reviews. Ages 11 to 15

New Moon: The Magazine for Girls and Their Dreams
34 E. Superior St., Ste. 200
Duluth, MN 55802–3003
www.newmoon.org/magazine/writerGirl.htm
Stories, articles, poems. Girls, ages 8 to 14

Scholastic Writing Contests
557 Broadway
New York, NY 10012
www.scholastic.com/artandwritingawards/enter.htm
Various categories; write or check Web site for details. Students, grades 7 to 12

Skipping Stones
P.O. Box 3939
Eugene, OR 97403–0939
www.skippingstones.org
Stories, essays, riddles, proverbs, and so on. Ages 8 to 16

Markets for the Writing of Students *(continued)*

Stone Soup
P.O. Box 83
Santa Cruz, CA 95063
www.stonesoup.com
Stories, poems, book reviews. Ages through 13

Teen Ink
P.O. Box 30
Newton, MA 02461
www.teenink.com
Stories, articles, poems, interviews, book reviews, movie reviews, video reviews, concert reviews, and so on. Ages 13 to 19

Teen Voices
c/o Women Express, Inc.
P.O. Box 120–027
Boston, MA 02112–0027
www.teenvoices.com/tvhome.html
Writings by teen girls, ages 13 to 19

The Apprentice Writer
Writer's Institute Director
Susquehanna University
Selinsgrove, PA 17870–1001
www.susqu.edu/writers/apprentice.htm
Stories, poems, essays, drama. Students, grades 9 to 12

Young Voices Magazine
P.O. Box 2321
Olympia, WA 98507
www.youngvoicesmagazine.com/
Stories, articles, poetry. Students from elementary through high school

ON-LINE MARKETS

Cyberkids
www.cyberkids.com
Various writings by kids, ages 7 to 12

Cyberteens
www.cyberteens.com
Various writings by teens, ages 13 to 17

Markets for the Writing of Students *(continued)*

Jupiter Sky Magazine
P.O. Box 45
Vienna, VA 22183
www.jupitersky.com
Stories, essays, fiction. Students, grades 9 to 12 and college

KidsOnlineMagazine
KidsOnlineMagazine.com
3405 Palm Avenue
Texas City, TX 77590
www.kidsonlinemagazine.com
Stories, articles, poetry, and so on. Ages through 18

The Magicoul's Nook
www.magicoul.com
Stories, articles, poetry. Ages 10 to 14

Note that local newspapers and regional magazines, which publish the material of students, can be additional markets.

Web Sites for Student Writers

The Internet offers a truly incredible amount of information for writers of all ages. The following list and their links provide plenty to keep young writers and their browsers busy.

Amazing Kids: www.amazing-kids.org/contests.htm

Dr. Grammar: www.drgrammar.org/

Kidnews: www.kidnews.com

KidPub: www.KidPub.com

Kids Courier: www.kidscourier.com/

PBS Kids: http://pbskids.org/bts/

Word Dance: www.worddance.com

Young Writer's Clubhouse: www.realkids.com/club.shtml

Youth Weekly: www.youthweekly.com

To find more Web sites for young writers, go to Yahooligans at www.yahooligans.com. In the search box, type "writing" or similar keywords and you will be directed to numerous sites about writing and writers.

Following are on-line reference sites that can be helpful to student writers.

Internet Public Library: www.ipl.org

Internet Public Library/Youth Division: www.ipl.org/div/kidspace

On-line dictionaries: www.dictionary.com

Roget's Thesaurus: www.thesaurus.com

Note: Many Internet service providers have links to comprehensive reference materials.

Writer's Glossary

Like other professions, writing has a special vocabulary of words that are unique to its field. Following are some.

advance – money paid to a writer by a publisher before a book is published; the money is charged against the royalties that the book will earn.

agent – a person who acts on the behalf of authors and tries to sell the author's writing. Agents receive a commission for their work.

anthology – a collection of selected writings, usually of various authors.

assignment – a situation in which an editor asks an author to write a specific article, story, or book.

author's tour – a "tour" in which an author visits various cities to promote a book.

B & W – an abbreviation for black-and-white photographs.

bimonthly – a publication that comes out every two months.

bionote – a sentence or short paragraph about an author that appears at the beginning of his or her article or story.

blurb – a brief publicity notice on a book jacket designed to arouse interest.

byline – the name of the author on published material.

caption – a written description of a photograph.

circulation – the number of subscribers to a magazine or newsletter.

clean copy – a manuscript that is free of errors and cross-outs.

clips – samples of a writer's published work.

column inch – the type contained in one inch of a typeset column.

contributor's copies – copies of a magazine sent to an author in which his or her work appears.

copy – a manuscript; also may refer to written material.

copyediting – the editing of a manuscript for mechanics (grammar, punctuation, and spelling) as well as for printing style.

copyright – the legal means of protecting the ownership of an author's work.

copywriting – the writing of material for advertising.

cover letter – a brief letter that accompanies the submission of a manuscript.

desktop publishing – publishing done using a personal computer.

docudrama – a fictionalized film based on actual, usually recent, events and real people.

editor – a person who accepts or rejects manuscripts for publication; editors also ensure that accepted manuscripts are prepared for publication.

electronic submission – material sent to an editor via the Internet or on a computer disk.

e-mail – electronic mail sent on a computer network or the Internet.

fair use – a provision of the copyright law that allows brief passages from copyrighted material to be used without violating the owner's rights.

feature – the lead article in a magazine.

filler – a short item used to "fill" leftover space in a magazine or newspaper.

freelance – a situation in which an author sells his or her material to various publishers.

genre – a classification of writing; science fiction, for example, is a genre.

ghostwriter – a writer who anonymously writes a book, article, or story for another.

glossy – a black-and-white photograph with a shiny surface.

how-to – a book or article that explains how to do something.

illustrations – photographs or artwork that accompany a manuscript.

interactive fiction – stories in which the reader chooses the way a story develops.

Internet – a global network of computers that provides access to electronic information.

kill fee – the fee paid for an article that was assigned and written but was not used.

mainstream fiction – popular fiction such as romance, mystery, or science fiction.

manuscript – a typed (prepublication) copy of a book, article, story, or poem.

model release – a consent signed by a person giving a photographer permission to use a photograph in which the person appears.

multiple submissions – the act of sending the same manuscript to several publishers at the same time.

newsbreak – an important story added to the front page of a newspaper or magazine at press time.

novel – a fictional book.

novella – a short novel.

paperback – a book that has a flexible paper binding.

payment on acceptance – a payment method in which a publisher pays a writer upon the editor's acceptance of the writer's work.

payment on publication – a payment method in which the writer is paid when his or her material is published.

pen name – a name other than his or her own that an author uses for publication (*also* nom de plume or pseudonym).

permission – a written consent that grants an author the right to use material originally published by another writer.

photo feature – an article in which the emphasis is on photographs rather than on written material.

plagiarism – the taking of the work of another writer and calling it one's own (or implying that it is one's own by not attributing it to another source).

print run – the number of books produced at a given printing.

proofreading – reading a manuscript to correct errors in mechanics.

proposal – a portion of a book used to interest a publisher, typically including an outline and sample chapters.

public domain – material on which the copyright term has expired, or material that was never copyrighted.

publisher – an individual or company that prints articles, stories, books, or poems.

query – a letter sent to an editor by a writer in which the writer tries to interest the editor in an idea for an article or story.

rejection – the unhappy situation that occurs when an editor decides not to accept or purchase a manuscript for publication.

royalties – payment to an author based on the amount of sales his or her book has achieved.

SASE – self-addressed, stamped envelope.

screenplay – a story written in a movie or TV format.

self-publish – the act of assuming the cost and production of one's own work.

serial – a newspaper or magazine (also stories in them) that appear at periodic intervals.

short-short – a story of between 250 and 1,500 words.

short story – a story that is relatively short in length.

sidebar – an additional, usually short, article that accompanies and highlights a feature.

slant – the design or development of an article or story that makes it suited to a particular audience.

slice-of-life story – short fiction that shows an interesting aspect of everyday life.

slush pile – the pile of unsolicited manuscripts received by an editor or publisher.

speculation – a situation in which an editor agrees to look at a manuscript with no commitment that he or she will buy it; often referred to as "on spec."

style – the manner in which a story or article is written; for example, in short, snappy sentences or long, flowing prose.

submission – the act of sending a manuscript to an editor.

synopsis – a brief summary of a novel, story, or play.

tagline – a comment added to a filler.

tear sheet – a page from a newspaper or magazine that contains an author's printed material.

trade – books sold primarily through general bookstores.

treatment – a detailed narrative outline for a proposed screenplay.

unsolicited manuscript – a manuscript that an editor or publisher receives but did not request.

vanity press – publishers who charge authors for the cost to produce the author's work.

YA – young adult books.

The Writing Process

Writing is a process composed of five major stages. It is a process in which the writer moves back and forth through the various stages. Following are the stages of the writing process, along with possible activities in which the writer may engage.

Stages	Possible Activities
I. Prewriting	finding ideas
	selecting a topic
	identifying a purpose
	brainstorming
	researching
	clarifying
	focusing a topic
	clustering
	analyzing
	organizing
	interviewing
	writing outlines
	writing leads
	illustrating
	freewriting
II. Writing the Draft	writing
	thinking
	rearranging
	alternating between writing and reading
	elaborating
	pausing
	planning
III. Revising	polishing
	rethinking
	rearranging
	clarifying
	rewriting
	more researching
	critiquing

The Writing Process *(continued)*

Stages	Possible Activities
IV. Editing	proofreading
	final polishing
	correcting mechanics
V. Publishing	submitting to magazines, newsletters, newspapers
	submitting to classroom or school publications
	readings
	displays
	bulletin boards
	exhibits

Bibliography Format

Writers include a bibliography to identify the sources they used when writing an article or book. Bibliographic entries are alphabetized according to the authors' last names. The title (underlined or italicized) of the book is next, followed by the place of publication, publisher, and copyright date. If the entire work was used, it is not necessary to cite page numbers; however, if only part of the work was used, page numbers should be noted. Anonymous bibliographical entries begin with the title. *Note:* Many publishers prefer a particular style, so be sure to check, but some samples of bibliographic style are given below.

BOOK, ONE AUTHOR

Hoffman, David. *Who Knew? Things You Didn't Know About Things You Know Well.* New York: MJF Books, 2000.

BOOK, TWO OR THREE AUTHORS

Ornstein, Robert, and Richard F. Thompson. *The Amazing Brain.* Boston: Houghton Mifflin, 1984, pp. 45–72.

BOOK, MORE THAN THREE AUTHORS

Dolciani, Mary P., et al. *Algebra: Structure and Method, Book 1.* Boston: Houghton Mifflin, 1980.

BOOK, A LATER EDITION

Henderson, Kathy. *The Young Writer's Guide to Getting Published* (6th ed.). Cincinnati: Writer's Digest Books, 2001, pp. 23–29.

BOOK, EDITED ANTHOLOGY

Weintraub, Pamela (Ed.). *The Omni Interviews.* Boston: Houghton Mifflin, 1984.

ARTICLE IN A REFERENCE BOOK

"Ecology." *The World Book Encyclopedia,* Vol. 6. Chicago: World Book, 1998, pp. 53–57.

ARTICLE IN A MONTHLY MAGAZINE

Mason, Betsy. "Season of Fire." *Discover* (Feb. 2003), pp. 32–39.

ARTICLE IN A WEEKLY MAGAZINE

Benjamin, Matthew. "Fads for Any and All Eras." *U.S. News and World Report* (Feb. 24–March 3, 2003), pp. 74–75.

ARTICLE IN A DAILY NEWSPAPER

Chira, Susan. "Electronic Teacher: A Mississippi Experiment." *The New York Times* (Jan. 24, 1990), p. A1.

Footnote/Endnote Format

Authors use footnotes or endnotes (notes at the end of a chapter or book instead of at the foot of the page) to identify the sources of quotations, to give credit to the authors of other works, and to provide supplementary information in their work. There are many formats for notes. Sometimes writers will offer complete bibliographical data with their notes. This is especially true when a separate bibliography is not included. When an article, book, or report contains a bibliography, a practical footnote/endnote format to follow includes the author's name, title, and pages.

BOOK, ONE AUTHOR

Joan Detz, *How to Write and Give a Speech,* p. 56.

BOOK, TWO OR THREE AUTHORS

Robert Ornstein and Richard F. Thompson, *The Amazing Brain,* p. 25.

BOOK, MORE THAN THREE AUTHORS

Mary P. Dolciani et al., *Algebra: Structure and Method, Book 1,* p. 87.

BOOK, A LATER EDITION

John B. Noss, *Man's Religions,* 4th ed., p. 119.

BOOK, EDITED ANTHOLOGY

Pamela Weintraub (Ed.), *The Omni Interviews,* p. 10.

ARTICLE IN A REFERENCE BOOK

"Ecology," *The World Book Encyclopedia,* Vol. 6 (1998), p. 53.

ARTICLE IN A MONTHLY MAGAZINE

Betsy Mason, "Season of Fire," *Discover* (Feb. 2003), p. 32.

ARTICLE IN A WEEKLY MAGAZINE

Matthew Benjamin, "Fads for Any and All Eras," *U.S. News and World Report* (Feb. 24–March 3, 2003), p. 74.

ARTICLE IN A DAILY NEWSPAPER

Susan Chira, "Electronic Teacher: A Mississippi Experiment," *The New York Times* (Jan. 24, 1990), p. A1.

Formats for Citing Electronic Sources

Electronic reference sources have become increasingly valuable to writers. As with print references, documentation is essential. While various standards of documentation are currently used, the following examples serve as acceptable formats for most people. In instances where the author's name is unavailable, start the entry with the title of the work.

ON-LINE MAGAZINE ARTICLE

Author's Last Name, First Name. "Title of Article." *Name of Magazine.* Month, day, year. (Online). URL or how to access.

ON-LINE NEWSPAPER ARTICLE

Author's Last Name, First Name. "Title of Article." *Name of Newspaper.* Edition. Month, day, year. (On-line). URL or how to access.

ON-LINE REFERENCE

"Title." Name of reference, version. Month, day, year. (On-line). URL or how to access.

CD-ROM PROGRAM

Author's Last Name, First Name. "Title of CD Program." Edition. (CD-ROM). Producer, year. Where to obtain or how to access.

EXAMPLE OF FORM FOR ON-LINE REFERENCE ARTICLE

"Atmosphere." *Encyclopaedia Britannica,* 2003. February 27, 2003. (Encyclopaedia Britannica Premium Service Online). http://www.britannica.com/eb/article?eu=18221

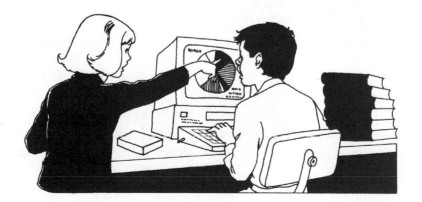

Books for Students About Writers and Writing

The following books offer student authors insight, inspiration, and tips on the craft of writing. Those titles followed by a YA have been written for young adults with the reading level being appropriate for grades 6 and up. The other titles are more suitable for high school students.

Bradford, Karleen. *Write Now! How to Turn Your Ideas into Great Stories.* Scholastic, 1996.

Brizzi, Mary T. *Anne McCaffrey.* Starmont House, 1986.

Bucknall, Barbara. *Ursula K. LeGuin.* Ungar, 1981.

Clark, Tom. *Jack Kerouac.* Harcourt Brace Jovanovich, 1984.

Clark, Tom. *The World of Damon Runyon.* Harper and Row, 1978.

Cleary, Beverly. *A Girl from Yamhill: A Memoir.* William Morrow, 1988. (YA)

Daly, Jay. *Presenting S.E. Hinton.* Twayne Publishers, 1987.

Donaldson, Scott. *John Cheever.* Random House, 1987.

Dubrovin, Vivian. *Write Your Own Story.* Watts, 1984. (YA)

Dunn, Jessica, and Danielle Dunn. *A Teen's Guide to Getting Published.* Prufrock Press, 1997. (YA)

Elledge, Scott. *E.B. White: A Biography.* Norton, 1984.

Ellis, Sarah. *The Young Writer's Companion.* Groundwood Books, 1999. (YA)

Fitch, Sheree. *Writing Maniac: How I Grew Up to Be a Writer (and You Can Too!).* Pembroke Publishers, 2001. (YA)

Gardner, John. *The Art of Fiction: Notes on Craft for Young Writers.* Vintage Books, 1985.

Garson, Helen S. *Truman Capote.* Ungar, 1980.

Grant, Janet E. *The Young Person's Guide to Becoming a Writer.* Free Spirit Press, 1995. (YA)

Greenfield, Howard. *F. Scott Fitzgerald.* Crown, 1974. (YA)

Haines, Charles. *Edgar Allan Poe: His Writings and Influence.* Watts, 1974. (YA)

Hamilton, Ian. *In Search of J.D. Salinger.* Random House, 1988.

Henderson, Kathy. *The Young Writer's Guide to Getting Published* (6th ed.). Writer's Digest Books, 2001. (YA)

Janeczko, Paul B. *Poetry from A to Z: A Guide for Young Writers.* Atheneum, 1994. (YA)

Kaplan, Justin. *Mark Twain and His World.* Crescent Books, 1982.

Lee, Betsy. *Judy Blume's Story.* Dillon, 1981. (YA)

Morgan, Janet P. *Agatha Christie: A Biography.* Knopf, 1985.

O'Connor, Richard. *Jack London: A Biography.* Little, 1964.

O'Hara, Mary. *Flicka's Friend: The Autobiography of Mary O'Hara.* Putnam, 1982.

O'Reilly, Timothy. *Frank Herbert.* Ungar, 1981. (YA)

Platt, Charles. *Dream Makers: Science Fiction and Fantasy Writers at Work.* Ungar, 1987. (YA)

Reynolds, Michael S. *The Young Hemingway.* Blackwell, 1986.

Sullivan, Wilson. *New England Men of Letters.* Macmillan, 1972. (YA)

Common Abbreviations

Abbreviations are shortened forms of words. Because they are used so much, it is helpful to know the ones that are used the most. Two sublists are included: "Days of the Week" and "Months." Note that while most abbreviations require periods, some do not.

A.D. – Anno Domini (in the year of our Lord)	elec. – electric
A.M. – ante meridiem (before noon)	et al. – et alii (and others)
acct. – account	etc. – et cetera (and others)
amt. – amount	ex. – example
anon. – anonymous	exec. – executive
ans. – answer	fig. – figure
assn. – association	fl oz – fluid ounce
asst. – assistant	ft – foot
atty. – attorney	g – gram
B.A. – Bachelor of Arts	gal – gallon
B.C. – before Christ	govt. – government
B.S. – Bachelor of Science	Hon. – honorable
bib. – bibliography	hosp. – hospital
biog. – biography	hp – horsepower
bldg. – building	hr – hour
Blvd. – boulevard	Hwy. – highway
cap. – capital	i.e. – id est (that is)
cc – cubic centimeter	ibid. – ibidem (in the same place)
chap. – chapter	illus. – illustration
cm – centimeter	in. – inch
Co. – company	Inc. – incorporated
Corp. – corporation	Jour. – journal
cu – cup	Jr. – junior
dept. – department	kg – kilogram
diam. – diameter	kl – kiloliter
div. – division	km – kilometer
doz. – dozen	l – liter
Dr. – doctor, drive	lat. – latitude
e.g. – exempli gratia (for example)	lb – pound
ea. – each	Ln. – lane
ed. – edition	long. – longitude
Ed.D. – Doctor of Education	m – meter

Common Abbreviations *(continued)*

M.A. – Master of Arts
M.B.A. – Master of Business Administration
M.D. – Doctor of Medicine
mdse. – merchandise
med. – medium
mg – milligram
min. – minute
misc. – miscellaneous
ml – milliliter
mm – millimeter
mo. – month
mph – miles per hour
Mr. – Mister
Mrs. – Mistress (married woman)
neg. – negative
opp. – opposite
oz – ounce
p. – page
P.M. – post meridiem (afternoon)
pd. – paid
Ph.D. – Doctor of Philosophy
pkg. – package
pl. – plural
pop. – population
pos. – positive
pp. – pages
Pres. – President
prin. – principal

pt – pint
qt – quart
R.N. – Registered Nurse
Rd. – road
recd. – received
ref. – referee, reference
Rev. – Reverend
sec. – second
sing. – singular
Sr. – senior
St. – saint, street
subj. – subject
Supt. – superintendent
T – ton
tbsp – tablespoon
tel. – telephone
tsp – teaspoon
univ. – university
USA – United States of America
vet. – veteran, veterinarian
vocab. – vocabulary
vol. – volume
wk. – week
wt. – weight
yd. – yard
yr. – year
zool. – zoology

DAYS OF THE WEEK

Sun. – Sunday
Mon. – Monday
Tues. – Tuesday
Wed. – Wednesday
Thurs. – Thursday
Fri. – Friday
Sat. – Saturday

MONTHS OF THE YEAR

Jan. – January
Feb. – February
Mar. – March
Apr. – April
Jul. – July

Aug. – August
Sept. – September
Oct. – October
Nov. – November
Dec. – December

Note: May and June are not usually abbreviated.

State Postal Abbreviations

The following postal abbreviations are essential for anyone who writes letters or addresses envelopes, and most especially for writers.

Alabama – AL

Alaska – AK

Arizona – AZ

Arkansas – AR

California – CA

Colorado – CO

Connecticut – CT

Delaware – DE

Florida – FL

Georgia – GA

Hawaii – HI

Idaho – ID

Illinois – IL

Indiana – IN

Iowa – IA

Kansas – KS

Kentucky – KY

Louisiana – LA

Maine – ME

Maryland – MD

Massachusetts – MA

Michigan – MI

Minnesota – MN

Mississippi – MS

Missouri – MO

Montana – MT

Nebraska – NE

Nevada – NV

New Hampshire – NH

New Jersey – NJ

New Mexico – NM

New York – NY

North Carolina – NC

North Dakota – ND

Ohio – OH

Oklahoma – OK

Oregon – OR

Pennsylvania – PA

Rhode Island – RI

South Carolina – SC

South Dakota – SD

Tennessee – TN

Texas – TX

Utah – UT

Vermont – VT

Virginia – VA

Washington – WA

West Virginia – WV

Wisconsin – WI

Wyoming – WY

Washington (District of Columbia) – DC

Common Initializations and Acronyms

In everyday language, it is common for some phrases to be used more often than others. When this happens, the initials of the phrases may become used as a short form of speaking or writing the phrase. Not only does this save time, but it allows the phrase to take on added emphasis. Initializations are usually written without periods after the letters. Similar to initializations, acronyms are shortened forms of phrases. Usually formed from the first letters of the words of the phrases, they are pronounced as words themselves. Periods are not used. Initializations and acronyms follow in two sublists.

COMMON INITIALIZATIONS

AKA – also known as

ASAP – as soon as possible

ATM – automated teller machine

BLT – bacon, lettuce, and tomato (sandwich)

CEO – chief executive officer (of a company)

COD – cash on delivery

CPA – certified public accountant

DA – district attorney

DJ – disk jockey

DOA – dead on arrival

ERA – Equal Rights Amendment

ESL – English as a second language

FYI – for your information

GNP – gross national product

HIV – human immunodeficiency virus

HMO – health maintenance organization

HQ – headquarters

IOU – I owe you

IQ – intelligence quotient

LIFO – last in, first out

MIA – missing in action

MO – modus operandi

MRI – magnetic resonance imaging

MYOB – mind your own business

PA – public address

PDQ – pretty darn quick

POW – prisoner of war

Common Initializations and Acronyms *(continued)*

PR – public relations

PTA – parent/teacher association

RIP – rest in peace

RSVP – repondez s'il vous plait (please reply)

RV – recreational vehicle

SASE – self-addressed, stamped envelope

SUV – sport utility vehicle

TBA – to be announced or arranged

TGIF – thank God it's Friday

TLC – tender loving care

TV – television

UFO – unidentified flying object

VCR – video cassette recorder

VIP – very important person

COMMON ACRONYMS

AIDS – acquired immune deficiency syndrome

AMEX – American Stock Exchange; American Express

AWOL – absent without leave

KISS – keep it simple, stupid

MADD – Mother's Against Drunk Driving

NASA – National Aeronautics and Space Administration

NATO – North Atlantic Treaty Organization

NIMBY – not in my backyard

OPEC – Organization of Petroleum Exporting Countries

OSHA – Occupational Safety and Health Administration

RADAR – radio detecting and ranging

SCUBA – self-contained underwater breathing apparatus

SNAFU – situation normal all fouled up

SONAR – sound navigation ranging

SWAK – sealed with a kiss

SWAT – special weapons action team

TEFLON – tetrafloroethylene resin

UNESCO – United Nations Educational, Scientific, and Cultural Organization

UNICEF – United Nations International Children's Emergency Fund

WASP – white Anglo-Saxon Protestant

ZIP – Zone Improvement Plan

Plagiarism and How to Avoid It

Plagiarism is taking the words or expression of ideas of another author and claiming that they are one's own. It is a type of theft that applies to all forms of writing and is a violation of the copyright laws.

To avoid plagiarism you should use your own words in your writing and present ideas in fresh ways. When it is necessary to borrow material from other writers, be sure to footnote the material or otherwise attribute it. If you use more than about fifty words from another source in something you plan to publish, you may seek permission from the original publisher to do so.

Always properly note the following:

- Direct quotes. Set them off with quotation marks. Never alter direct quotes unless you indicate you have done so.

- Specific ideas taken from another source. Even if rewritten in your words, specific ideas should be noted.

- The opinions of others, whether directly quoted or paraphrased.

- Any specific display of facts, such as charts, tables, or diagrams.

See List 73, "Bibliography Format," List 74, "Footnote/Endnote Format," and List 75, "Formats for Citing Electronic Sources."

Steps for Doing a Research Paper

Following are ten steps that can act as guideposts in the completion of a research paper.

1. Select and limit your subject. Choose a subject that you find interesting, then do general background reading to gain an understanding of the scope of the material. Narrow your subject down to a well-focused topic.

2. Decide what sources you will need. Will you require books, on-line references, magazines, interviews, or forms of nonprint media such as tapes or photographs? Where will you find these sources?

3. Prepare a preliminary outline. This may be merely a list of the main ideas or topics that will appear in your paper, but it will guide you in your research efforts.

4. Conduct your research. Take accurate notes, and record your sources, including page references. This will save much time later.

5. Review your notes. Analyze, combine, and organize your information. If necessary, conduct further research.

6. Organize your information into an outline. Remember that every research paper consists of three basic parts: an introduction, a body, and a conclusion.

7. Write your first draft. Follow your outline for this.

8. Make sure that you support all major ideas with facts and examples.

9. Review and revise your draft. Make any additions or deletions as well as polish the writing.

10. Write the final copy, making any final changes.

11. Include footnotes and a bibliography.

Note: When printing your work, use 8.5 by 11-inch white paper, print on only one side with black ink, and use double spacing. Extended quotes should be single-spaced. Be sure to leave ample margins.

Ways to Improve Your Scores on Writing Tests

The following suggestions can help you boost your scores on writing tests.

1. Be prepared. Make sure you are familiar with any test topics your teacher provides. Studying not only helps you to gain knowledge about possible topics, but it also builds confidence.

2. Get a good night's sleep the night before the test. Wake up on time and eat a solid breakfast. This will help you to concentrate during the test.

3. During the test, think positively and remain calm. People who have prepared and believe they will do well on writing tests usually do better than those who worry and expect to do poorly.

4. Listen carefully to all directions and follow them exactly. If you don't understand something, ask your teacher.

5. If you have a choice of questions, read them all to determine which one(s) you are best able to answer.

6. Read each question carefully. Be certain you know exactly what it is asking. Look for key words such as *summarize, describe, explain, compare, contrast, analyze,* and *discuss.*

7. Write your ideas down on scrap paper, if possible, and organize them in a logical manner. As you do, look for connections and relationships between ideas.

8. As you write, be sure to stay on the topic. Support your ideas with facts and examples. Keep your writing concise.

9. Budget your time. Work quickly and thoroughly, but keep in mind that most tests come with time limits sufficient for students to finish.

10. Do your best. If time remains, reread your work and make any final changes.

SPECIAL LISTS FOR
Teachers

Promoting the "Write" Atmosphere

Establishing a writer's environment in your classroom can be of great help in teaching students to write effectively. Following are some things to consider.

- Maintain a positive environment that encourages the sharing of ideas.

- Encourage students to write about meaningful topics and subjects.

- Treat writing as a process composed of several stages: prewriting, drafting, revising, editing, and publishing.

- Make your classroom bright and cheerful. Select posters and displays that stimulate the mind.

- Encourage students to write in journals each day.

- Encourage students to maintain idea folders into which they can store ideas, puzzling questions, newspaper clippings, or musings that they can refer to later.

- Never accept that students have no ideas for writing; ideas are everywhere.

- Foster the attitude that imagination is an important ability, and like any ability it can be improved through use.

- Encourage experimentation with literary forms.

- Encourage the acquisition of spelling, grammar, and usage skills within the process of writing.

- Link writing to literature. Let students know that great books are the result of great writing.

- Provide dictionaries, thesauruses, rhyming dictionaries, grammar references, and stylebooks.

- Publish and share the writings of your students.

Books and Resources About Teaching Writing

Writing is one of the most difficult subjects to teach. While there are numerous books on the subject, the following can be especially helpful.

Atwell, Nanci. *In the Middle: New Understanding about Writing, Reading, and Learning.* Boynton/Cook, 1998.

Calkins, Lucy. *The Art of Teaching Writing.* Heinemann, 1986.

Graves, Donald H. *Writing: Teachers and Children at Work.* Heinemann, 1983.

Graves, Donald H. *A Fresh Look at Writing.* Heinemann, 1994.

Hillerich, Robert. *Teaching Children to Write, K-8.* Prentice Hall, 1985.

Muschla, Gary Robert. *Writing Workshop Survival Kit.* Jossey-Bass, 1993.

National Writing Project and Carl Nagin. *Because Writing Matters: Improving Student Writing in Our Schools.* John Wiley & Sons, 2003.

Padgett, Ron (Ed.). *The Teachers and Writers Handbook of Poetic Forms.* Teachers and Writers Collaborative, 1987.

Perl, Sondra, and Nancy Wilson. *Through Teacher's Eyes: Portraits of Writing Teachers at Work.* Heinemann, 1986.

Piazza, Carolyn. *Journeys: The Teaching of Writing in the Elementary Classroom.* Prentice Hall, 2002.

Reid, Joy M. *Teaching ESL Writing.* Pearson, 1993.

Romano, Tom. *Clearing the Way: Working with Teenage Writers.* Heinemann, 1987.

Soven, Margot Iris. *Teaching Writing in Middle and Secondary Schools: Theory, Research, and Practice.* Allyn and Bacon, 1998.

Strunk, William, and E.B. White. *The Elements of Style* (4th ed.). Longman, 2000.

Zemelman, Steven, and Harvey Daniels. *A Community of Writers: Teaching Writing in the Junior and Senior High School.* Heinemann, 1988.

Zinsser, William. *On Writing Well* (4th ed.). Harper and Row, 1990.

Grading the Writing of Your Students

Grading the writing of students is always a difficult task. The following material includes general keys for effective grading, guidelines for determining grades based on point totals, and a skills chart. Teachers may complete the chart after each assignment and record major strengths and weaknesses. Skills charts provide an excellent record of writing progress over the year.

KEYS TO EFFECTIVE GRADING

- Grading should help rather than hinder.

- Evaluation should not be merely a form of criticism.

- Grades cannot take the place of written suggestions or conferences.

- Evaluation should reflect what has been taught.

- Grading should be based on the whole piece.

- Grading should be consistent from student to student.

- Students should know ahead of time how grades will be determined.

- Report-card grades should be based on an average of a student's best three or four papers. This takes into account that all writers vary in the quality of their work. (You may allow students to select what they consider to be their best work.)

GRADING WRITING—POINT TOTALS

Some teachers prefer to use percentages for grading. Following is a suggestion for assigning point totals to different parts of students' writing.

- *Focus:* The topic is clearly defined. (10 pts.)

- *Content:* The student uses fresh, insightful, or original ideas; the ideas are developed and relate to the topic. (25 pts.)

- *Organization:* The piece progresses logically from beginning to end. It possesses an identifiable introduction, body, and conclusion. Main ideas are supported with details. (25 pts.)

- *Mechanics:* Correct punctuation, grammar, usage, spelling, and paragraphing are used. (20 pts.)

- *Imagery:* Precise, colorful words that paint vivid pictures in the mind of the reader are used. (10 pts.)

- *Style:* The overall writing is clear and has a distinct sense of individuality. (10 pts.)

Name _____   Date _____

Assignment _____

SKILL	COMMENTS	POINTS
FOCUS		
CONTENT		
ORGANIZATION		
MECHANICS		
IMAGERY		
STYLE		
OTHER		

Questions to Help Focus Writing Topics

One of the biggest problems students have with writing is discovering the full scope of their subjects. The following questions are designed to help you guide young writers in the examination of their subjects so that they can understand their material as well as possible. This will enable them to write more effectively on their topics.

1. Examine the subject.

   - Define the subject. What exactly is it? What does it include?

   - Describe the subject. What is it like? Does it have parts? How is it similar to other things? How is it different from other things?

   - What is the purpose of the subject? What does it do?

   - Why is the subject important? Why is it worthy to write about?

2. Examine the subject in relation to other things.

   - How did the subject develop? How did it arise?

   - What things is the subject related to? What things does it affect? What things affect it? What changes does it bring about in other things?

   - Is the subject a part of something bigger? How? Do smaller things make it up? How?

   - Does the subject follow something? What is it? What comes after the subject?

   - Does the subject have an opposite? How does this opposite affect the subject?

3. Examine the value of the subject.

   - Does the subject have social value? How?

   - Does the subject have economic value? How?

   - Does the subject embody any great truths or principles? What are they?

   - Why might others want to know about the subject? What meaning might it have for others?

Writing Activities for Other Subjects

Writing should be a significant part of every class, not just language arts. When a school is committed to writing instruction, students gain significant exposure to writing forms and purposes. Every class can incorporate writing into its routines and lessons. Following is a list of activities.

WRITING FOR ART

- Paint self-portraits and write autobiographical sketches.

- Draw and describe in writing imaginary creatures.

- Write an article about moods and colors.

- Create a photo essay with captions for the photos.

- Design an imaginary object using clay or another material. Then write a story about it.

- Produce an object and write a set of instructions explaining how others can make it.

- Make puppets, write a script for a puppet show, and perform the show.

- Make a collage depicting an issue that has personal meaning and write an essay on the topic.

- Write and illustrate a tall tale.

- Write a science fiction story. Illustrate it or create an object that depicts some part of the story.

- Write, produce, and videotape a screenplay. (Organize a school student-film fest.)

WRITING FOR MATH

- Select famous mathematicians. Pythagoras is an example. Write biographies about the lives of these people, focusing on their mathematical accomplishments. Perhaps the biographies can be compiled into a class book of famous mathematicians.

- Write an essay entitled "Numbers: Why We Can't Do Without Them."

- Write word problems that other students solve. (This can be done throughout the year as different topics are covered.)

- Write articles about how mathematics affects our lives.

- Produce a mathematics newsletter containing information about the math goings-on of your school.

- Select a geometric figure—a square, triangle, or rectangle, for example—and write a poem or story about it.

- Create math puzzles and write directions how to solve them.

- Pretend to be a math teacher and write a dialogue in which you try to convince students of the importance of math.

WRITING FOR MUSIC

- Write a biography of a famous composer.

- Write songs and lyrics. (Your school may conduct a song-writing contest for students.)

- Choose a favorite singer. Imagine being able to go on tour with this star. What would it be like? Write an account of this imaginary experience.

- Write, create, and perform your own rock videos. (Your class may wish to tape the best ones or conduct a contest.)

- Write an editorial on why you should or should not be permitted to listen to the type of music you like.

- Select a type of music and write a report about it, including its origin, where it is most often played, and its unique elements.

WRITING FOR READING

- Select a favorite story and write a summary of it.

- Write book reviews. (Compile the reviews and use them in the selection of new books to read.)

- Read a play; then write a play of your own on a topic of your choice. (Allow students to create props and act out their plays.)

- Choose a favorite character and write a poem describing this character.

- Write biographies of famous authors.

- Choose a favorite story and write a new ending.

- Write essays comparing reading and television.

WRITING FOR SCIENCE

- Write a research report comparing science and superstition.

- Write an article about the importance of a balanced diet.

- Write a story based on a topic you have studied or are currently studying.

- Choose a mystery—some examples are UFOs, Bigfoot, the Loch Ness monster, and ghosts. Conduct the necessary research and write a report.

- Pretend to be a scientist and plan a trip to another planet. Describe your preparations in an essay or story.

- Imagine that aliens have made contact with Earth. Write an imaginary interview with the first alien to land on Earth.

- Select a famous scientist from the topic you are currently studying and write a biographical sketch.

- Create a model of a topic in science and write a description.

- Write an article entitled "Modern Methods in Weather Forecasting."

- Write articles describing possible energy sources of the future.

- Write a proposal for an experiment, detailing each step of the scientific process, particularly hypothesis, procedure, and controls.

- Write a summary of the results of an experiment.

WRITING FOR SOCIAL STUDIES

- Select a historical event, imagine you are a reporter at the scene, and write a news story describing the event.

- Choose a favorite product, and write a description of why it is good and worthwhile.

- Write a brochure that describes your town or neighborhood.

- Choose a topic of major importance—terrorism, poverty, homelessness, drug abuse— and write a report examining potential solutions.

- Imagine that time travel is possible. Write a travel brochure describing a vacation spot from the past or for the future.

- Select a problem or issue that is meaningful to you and write an editorial.

- Research and write a biography about a major historical figure you admire.

- Select a country from which one or more of your ancestors came. Compare that country with the United States.

Ways to Publish the Writing of Your Students

There are many ways to share, or publish, the writing of your students.

- Readings, in which students read excerpts of their work out loud in class.
- Bulletin boards in class.
- Hallway displays.
- Publication on class or school Web sites.
- Publication in class or school magazines or newsletters.
- Publication in PTA newsletters.
- Sharing writing with parents and asking for written comments.
- Photocopying writing and sharing with other students.
- Presenting writing to students of other classes.
- Producing class books of selected writing.
- Developing anthologies of student writing and displaying them in the school or local library.
- Submitting student writing to local newspapers.
- Submitting writing to magazines that publish the writing of students.
- Submitting writing to Web sites that publish the writing of students.

See List 69, "Markets for the Writing of Students," and List 70, "Web Sites for Student Writers."

Guidelines for Writer's Conferences

The writer's conference is a time for teaching and learning. Following are some suggestions to help you make your conferences more effective.

1. Set up a schedule and follow it. Some teachers prefer to meet with students after every assignment, while others prefer to meet regularly once every week or every few weeks. Adhering to a schedule allows both teacher and student to plan for the meeting.

2. Meet in a corner of the room, at your desk, at the student's desk, or in some other designated area.

3. If possible, begin the conference by asking your students what they wish to focus on. This is especially helpful when discussing a work in progress.

4. Keep your conferences short. A few minutes are usually sufficient. Rather than reading the entire piece during the conference, try to read it earlier and make notes. Use the conference time for talking and sharing.

5. Focus on one or two specific strengths and weaknesses of the piece. It is impossible to talk about the entire piece; even if you tried, you would likely overwhelm your students.

6. See every student. If you can't get to everyone one day, make sure you do as soon as you can.

7. Be sincere and specific in your praise. Students can see through false praise. When offering compliments on their writing, point out particular strengths. "Your imagery is strong. I can picture that old house clearly."

8. Be helpful with criticism. Avoid negative or sarcastic comments and instead use criticism as a way to help students improve their writing skills. Rather than "Your dialogue is poor because it lacks quotation marks," say "The reader needs to know when characters are speaking. The writer does this by using quotation marks."

9. Base your suggestions for improvement on skills that the student knows. Build on mastered skills.

10. Remember to listen to your students. Don't make the conference a one-way street. Ask students how they feel they might be able to improve the piece. What do they like about their writing? How do they feel they can improve? Establish a dialogue with your students so that they become partners with you in the development of their writing skills.

Self-Appraisal for Teachers of Writing

Answering the following questions can help you improve your writing classes and make them an exciting, challenging, and satisfying experience for your students.

- Are the procedures I have established clear, efficient, and supportive of a writing class?

- Do I maintain a positive atmosphere in my classes? How might I enhance the environment for writing?

- Do I gear my instruction to the needs and abilities of my students?

- Do I help students find topics for writing?

- Do I help students focus their topics?

- Do I answer students' questions about writing?

- Do I guide students in their research efforts?

- Do I help students organize their ideas?

- Do I offer help with revision?

- Do I provide my students with instruction that concentrates on specific writing skills?

- Do I confer with my students regularly?

- Do I use writing conferences efficiently?

- Do I provide time for individual, collaborative, and cooperative writing activities?

- Are my methods of evaluation fair and consistent?

- Do I always treat writing as an important subject?

Books of Interest by Gary Robert Muschla

Writing Workshop Survival Kit

ISBN: 0-87628-972-3

Paperback/ 272 pages/ 1993

The Writing Workshop Survival Kit, for English teachers and writing teachers in grades 5–12, is a comprehensive, step-by-step guide to teaching the writing process in a class workshop setting. The book is conveniently organized into two parts.

Part I, The Writing Process in the Writing Workshop, explains the writing workshop, offers specific strategies and tools for classroom management, and provides reproducible handouts and activities for each stage of the writing process, prewriting to publishing.

Part II, Using Mini-Lessons in the Writing Workshop, contains three different kinds of mini-lessons focusing on specific writing topics and skills. Each of these mini-lessons stands alone and can be implemented whenever you wish, and many are accompanied by reproducibles.

This book places at your fingertips more than 150 ready-to-use activities/lessons you can share with your students. They will give your students a variety of interesting writing experiences and help make your teaching in the writing workshop easier and more effective.

Reading Workshop Survival Kit

ISBN: 0-87628-592-2

Paperback/ 336 pages/ 1997

For reading and classroom teachers in grades 5–12, this is a complete, step-by-step guide to setting up and running successful reading workshops where reading is the priority. The Survival Kit is conveniently organized into two parts.

Part I, Management of the Reading Workshop, shows how to create a reading workshop, offers specific tools and strategies for classroom management, and includes reproducible handouts.

Part II, Using Mini-Lessons in the Reading Workshop, contains 100 different mini-lessons focusing on specific reading topics and skills. Each of the lessons stands alone, can be used in any order you wish, and is accompanied by one or two reproducibles.

60 Ready-to-Use Activity Packets Featuring
Classic, Popular & Current Literature

GARY ROBERT MUSCHLA

English Teacher's Great Books Activities Kit:

60 Ready-to-Use Activity Packets Featuring Classic, Popular & Current Literature

ISBN: 0-87628-854-9

Paperback/ 308 pages/ 1994

This resource gives English teachers in grades 7–12 practical management techniques and 60 ready-to-use activity packets containing over 180 reproducible student activities for teaching reading and writing skills through a variety of classic, popular, and current literature.

Each of these literature-based packets offers students the chance to learn language skills within the context of an entire story rather than in isolation, and these skills are easily correlated with other subjects across the curriculum. Each packet opens a new world of ideas and places to your students. The Kit is printed in a big 8-1/2" x 11" format that folds flat for easy photocopying of the student activity sheets and is organized into two sections:

Part I, Managing Your English Classes, identifies the elements of effective English classes and the role of literature, and provides specific guidelines and tools for managing reading, writing, and evaluation.

Part II, Ready-To-Use Activities, presents reproducible activity packets for 60 different novels, including 20 each for grades 7–8, grades 9–10, and grades 11–12.